Daily
Bread

Cindi Flahive-Sobel

A FIRESIDE BOOK

Published by Simon & Schuster

Daily Bread

*M*ORE

THAN 50 IRRESISTIBLE RECIPES

FOR LOW-FAT AND NO-FAT BREADS

AND MUFFINS, AND OTHER DELICIOUS,

EASY-TO-MAKE TREATS

FIRESIDE
Rockefeller Center
1230 Avenue of the Americas
New York, NY 10020

FIRESIDE and colophon are registered trademarks
of Simon & Schuster Inc.

Designed by Katy Riegel
Illustrations by Cindy Wrobel

Manufactured in the United States of America

1   3   5   7   9   10   8   6   4   2

Library of Congress Cataloging-in-Publication Data

Flahive-Sobel, Cindi.
Daily bread : 50 irresistible recipes for low-fat and no-fat
breads and muffins, and other delicious, easy-to-make treats / Cindi
Flahive-Sobel.
p.   cm.
"A Fireside book."
Includes index.
1. Bread.   2. Low-fat diet—Recipes.   I. Title.
TX769.F62   1996
641.8'15—dc20
96-27497
CIP

ISBN 0-684-80317-8

$\mathcal{A}$cknowledgments

Thank you to Sydny Miner for initiating this project and for having such a passion for breads. I also wish to acknowledge Evelyn and Bill Sobel for their financial support and Frank and JoAnne Flahive for their understanding of what determination really means. To Diane Sianowski for her help in recipe development and for running the stores with such grit and attitude. And to my very own nag, Scott Sobel, without whose constant irritation I might not hit any deadline.

To the ones who are my highest joys
and deepest agonies . . .
my children . . .
Colin, Conor, Corey,
Kylie and Killian

Contents

The Story of Boston Daily Bread   15

Ingredients   17

Equipment   21

Getting It Right   23

The "Good Dough"   27

Daily Bread   29

White Breads   31

Whole-Wheat Breads   55

Bread Machines   69

Muffins and Quick Breads   77

Orphans   91

Losing Our Way   99

Spreading the Wealth   115

Sources   123

Index   129

Metric Equivalencies   141

The Story of Boston Daily Bread

ONCE UPON A TIME in a state far, far away lived a mom who thought life was perfect. She had a husband who worked hard and made a lot of money (so it seemed for a girl who had never had much), five almost perfect children with varying degrees of minor neuroses and the proverbial "gifted" IQs that all children in her income group had, a home on a mountain with two new cars and the right amount of social consciousness to make her believe that because of her good works in the church, school, and her community at large, these gifts were all, of course, her due.

This was me. And one day my world came screeching to a stop. My husband was told that his position was not going to be around (after which someone fifteen years younger was hired at one-third of his salary) and we were staring down a strange road that we used to think was a well-planned future.

Our search began. We looked at work in his field (half the pay, no guarantees for the future), work in similar fields (not enough experience), work in smaller towns (too much experience), and met a lot of people who were going through the same struggle as ourselves. We woke up and found ourselves in the decade of downsizing. Then, on our friend Mary Jo O'Rourke's suggestion, we began to think about opening a bread store.

Not just any bread store, mind you, but one like those stores we'd frequented where the making of fat-free, all-natural products from freshly milled flour was taken quite for granted. These stores made what I had, for years, baked at home—cheese breads, sourdoughs, quick breads. We also liked to eat hearty, soft-crusted breads that reminded me of my growing-up years in Wisconsin, Colorado, and Montana. This was the business we wanted.

So our new life began. We started doing research, haunting these bakeries, hovering around taking pictures, tasting breads, asking questions, reading lots of books, and then going on trips around the country looking for just the right place to open our own bakery. What could it take to start a bakery? How hard could it be? Having been given lots of guts and not a lot of fear, it sounded like a great adventure!

And so, on a crisp September afternoon, on my second trip to Boston (where I thought we could all be happy), I found myself lost for the umpteenth time that day in Coolidge Corner in Brookline. And Boston Daily Bread had found a home. So we sold the house (burying a statue of Saint Francis in the front yard to get it sold is a book all by itself!), cashed in the kids' college money, begged a loan from my husband's parents, and put the kids, the dog, the bird, and the vacuum cleaner in our two cars and left our beloved Colorado.

Today, we have two stores, in Brookline and Sudbury, Massachusetts, and there are bakeries that share our recipes and philosophy all over the country (you'll find their names and addresses in the back of the book). In this book, you'll find the delicious results of our years of experience and experimentation, all adapted for, and tested in, kitchens like yours, using the ingredients that you can find in your local grocery and/or natural foods store. We've tested, retested, and tasted all these recipes, and have tried to provide you with extra tips and advice on baking with whole grains and little or no fat, so you can reproduce the smells and tastes of Boston Daily Bread in your home.

So roll up your sleeves and dig in. Enjoy the process and the end result, and welcome to Daily Bread!

Ingredients

HAVE YOU EVER OPENED a cookbook and read: "We want you to use only the cheapest, most disgustingly ill-conceived artificial food substitutes you can find in the store"? So let's just state the obvious again: Use good ingredients, get good bread. Use good ingredients, get good salad. Use good ingredients, get good anything. You decide the quality of the food that you want to put in your body and go from there.

Flour

The finest flour you can use is freshly ground from the finest wheat berries. Hard spring red and white wheat grown in the high altitudes of the Rocky Mountain region are the best wheats available. Wheat Montana Farms is, in my opinion, the most consistent producer, having used a no-till method for many years and producing all their grains with no chemicals whatsoever.

Absent this source, we recommend bread flour made with hard red or white wheat. All-purpose flour, a combination of hard and soft wheat, can be used interchangeably with bread flour and is acceptable for most of our recipes. Flour does go stale, so use it as you buy it. Keep it refrigerated or in the freezer, especially if you don't bake frequently.

Stone-ground whole-grain flour is milled slowly, using granite stones, which keeps the flour cooler than a steel milling system. If you have access to a local mill, they will often sell you flour from their old granite mill. In Sudbury, we have a famous grist mill that sits picturesquely across the road from Longfellow's Wayside Inn. The millwright, Rich, tells of the days when the parameters of communities were established by what mill serviced you and your family. Keep whole-grain flours refrigerated or in the freezer. Whole grains themselves will keep indefinitely stored in an air-tight container.

Rye is a strong-flavored grain that grows wild in parts of Europe. Since rye contains little gluten, rye and wheat flours are usually combined to get a lighter loaf. Medium rye flour is the best type to use in our recipes.

Cornmeal is used in several of our recipes. Coarsely ground cornmeal, both yellow and white, is ground from the whole corn kernel and makes yummy breads. We like the yellow cornmeal because the color contrast with ingredients like jalapeño peppers and olives makes an attractive presentation.

Leavening

Yeast is a living one-celled plant that is the life of breads. It interacts with sugar, liquid, and heat to produce the rising action in bread. Yeast, which can be killed at temperatures over 140°F and deactivated at temperatures below 50°F, is most active at temperatures between 95 and 105°F. We have adjusted the recipes for the use of refrigerated flour or heated ingredients.

Yeast comes in four different forms:

• *Fresh or compressed yeast* is very dependable and stable; it comes in foil-wrapped cakes. I love the feel and smell of cake yeast, but it has a limited shelf life. Check the dairy aisle in your supermarket, and be sure to check the expiration date. If you have a bakery in your area, stop in and ask the bakery if they will sell some to you.

• *Active dry yeast* is sold in packets, jars, or, in some co-ops, in bulk. One package is the same as a scant tablespoon. Bulk yeast must be stored in an air-tight, moisture-proof container. This type of yeast can last up to a year, but do check that expiration date. It's very frustrating to spend a morning baking and wind up with flat bread.

• *Quick-rise yeast* is a low-moisture yeast that rises twice as fast as regular yeast. It needs to be added directly to the dry ingredients, and the temperatures of liquids in the recipes should be raised about 15 degrees. If this is the only yeast available, decrease the amount of yeast by half when active dry yeast is called for.

• *Instant dried yeast* is combined with an emulsifier and a sugar source. I don't use it because the rising time is changed so dramatically. While this yeast will produce bread, too much flavor is lost in the process for it to be an acceptable choice for the recipes in this book.

Baking powder and **baking soda** are chemical leavening agents used for quick breads, muffins, and scones. Each has a different interaction with ingredients, and you cannot substitute one for the other. Measure these ingredients carefully; using too much or too little of either can produce some wacky results.

Sweeteners

Sweeteners both feed the yeast in bread and provide the sweetening. They also provide color to the crust. When we use sugar in a recipe, I will specify what type—that is, white, powdered, brown.

Most of our recipes are sweetened with **honey.** The character and flavor of honey is determined by the flowers and plants chosen by the bees who produce the honey, and vary greatly. The darker the honey, the browner the crust; a very dark honey can produce a crust that is overbrowned.

We use a light clover honey in our recipes; it has a mild flavor and a light to medium color.

When we call for **molasses** in a recipe we mean unsulfured molasses. Blackstrap or sulfured molasses is too thick and overpowering.

Salt

Salt has many functions in bread baking. In a yeasted loaf, it adds savor and enhances other flavors, as well as acting as a balance, or neutralizer, to the yeast. In many whole-grain breads, so much yeast is used in the sponge that a lot of salt is needed in the final mix. Sea salt can be substituted for table salt, iodized or not. All coarse salts should be ground fine before you use them.

$\mathcal{E}$quipment

THE EQUIPMENT FOR BAKING BREAD can be as simple as a bowl and an oven or as high tech as a programmable bread machine. Most of our recipes can be made by hand or mixed in a **heavy-duty standing mixer** with a dough hook. We used a Kitchen-Aid when we tested these recipes; it's a smaller version of the Hobart mixers that we use in our stores and produces a beautifully smooth, consistent dough. If you prefer another brand, that's fine, but don't try mixing these doughs with a hand mixer. Each recipe will specify the appropriate attachment used for each phase of the dough.

Mixing dough by hand requires a sturdy **bowl**, a **dishtowel** to throw over the top, and **measuring cups and spoons.** The rest is done with your own two hands.

The pans used for these recipes are standard **loaf pans,** 9×5×3 inches. If you prefer a "boule," or round loaf, place the dough on a **sheet pan** or **cookie sheet.** We use a 16-gauge or higher sheet in the stores; that means a heavy-duty cookie sheet. Using an insulated sheet pan means less crust on the bottom of the bread—it's a matter of personal preference. If you use a glass bread pan, lower the oven temperature by 25 degrees. You can also use clean one-pound **coffee cans** as bread pans. New England brown bread is traditionally prepared in this form.

Muffin tins vary in size from mini to Texas-size (jumbo), and even pans that just give you the muffin top! Remember to adjust the baking time according to the size of your tin—less time for the smaller muffins and longer for the bigger ones. Lightweight pans will warp, so use the heaviest pans you can find. Specialty cookware and restaurant supply stores are a good source.

Because we bake without added fats, we spray all our loaf pans and muffin tins with an aerosol **no-fat cooking spray** or pan release. Spray heavily if you are making a sweet bread and lightly for all others.

You'll need **measuring cups and spoons** to make sure your ingredients are measured accurately, and a **whisk** and **wooden spoons** come in handy for mixing liquid batters and sponges. A **thermometer** for taking the water temperature is nice, but you can bake a fine loaf without one.

A metal or **plastic dough scraper** or **rubber spatula** will help get your bowls and your work surface clean. A **rolling pin** will help you get doughs evenly spread for treats like cinnamon rolls, and a **pastry brush** will nicely spread the toppings on proofed dough.

Just remember, this is bread baking, not brain surgery. Don't let yourself be intimidated or inhibited because you don't have something on this list. Improvise! Use your hands! Soon you'll be able to measure the salt in the palm of your hand and your flour in a teacup, just like Grandma did. And it will be just right.

Getting It Right

As I TRAVEL AROUND the country (and soon around the world!) consulting to new bakery owners, I constantly repeat (as you've already read), "It isn't brain surgery, it's bread baking." I have trained airline pilots, attorneys, psychologists, even a nuclear engineer to be bakers, and they are all making terrific bread.

Just as with any other skill, you need to know what to watch for, how to identify a problem, and how to correct it if you're going to make good bread. Read this section before you begin baking.

First, you must measure carefully. Nine times out of ten, if a batch of dough is mixing poorly, the problem can be traced to a careless baker. My mother, from whom I learned to bake, never used measuring tools, but she had an sense of what the right proportions of ingredients for a dough were, and how to make adjustments to compensate for differences in ingredients. So will you—but not the first time out of the chute!

When you begin to mix the dough, it will appear sticky, then, after all the dry and wet ingredients are incorporated, you should start to see a dough ball form. (It's a good idea to keep part of the flour aside until the end, as it's always easier to "dry out" a dough by adding more flour than it is to add water.) This is when the gluten begins to develop. At this point, if you are using a mixer, you will continue to mix on medium to medium-high speed until you have a finished dough. If you are mixing by hand, take the dough to the kneading area, and without mixing in a lot more flour, knead until smooth. When you're finished, you should have an elastic, fairly smooth ball that should stretch a bit without tearing. (See "The 'Good Dough,'" page 27, for more information.)

When I first made bread, I was always anxious about whether the dough was "smooth" enough. Trust your instincts—dough doesn't become overdeveloped and tough (an "old dough") in an instant. Knead or mix it a bit longer if you're feeling unsure. If the dough begins to tear apart or you feel the elasticity becoming looser, or slackening, stop and put the dough aside.

When you let the bread rise, keep it covered with a moist (not soggy!) cloth in a warm, preferably draft-free place. A dough temperature of 80 to 85°F with high humidity is ideal. Setting the bowl over the pilot light of a gas stove or in a sunny window are both good situations.

Divide the dough by punching it down, cutting it in half with a sharp knife, and forming each half into a loaf in the shape that appeals to you. Each yeasted bread recipe makes two pan loaves or two boules (round loaves).

Don't be timid when you're forming the loaves. Do it with authority and speed, since overworking the dough tears the skin and makes the bread ugly. Rather than doing it over again and again until it's "perfect," get the air bubbles out as best you can and get the dough into the pans.

For pan loaves, flatten the dough out either by hand or with a rolling pin. Roll it up like a jelly roll or a sleeping bag, tucking in the ends, then place the loaves in the sprayed pans.

For boules, flatten the dough out by hand or with a rolling pin, and then bring the edges into the center, about a fifth at a time, working the outside dough into the middle. Use the bottom of the dough, or skin, to help form the round. Make it as round as you can (practice makes perfect—your first loaves may not look that great but they'll taste fine) and place the loaf on a sprayed large cookie sheet. Two loaves should fit on one sheet.

Remember—it takes time and experience to get the feel of the dough and to make an attractive loaf. I always suggest that my novice bakery owners sell the ugly loaves at a premium because they have special character! We named our white bread Peasant White because those first loaves were incredibly uneven and crude-looking when we first opened!

After dividing the dough and placing the loaves in pans or on the cookie sheet, the bread will "proof," or go through its final rise outside the oven. Preheat your oven, and let the bread sit, covered, on top of the stove until the dough is taut enough that when you touch it with your finger, the mark doesn't stay depressed. Now it's ready for the oven.

When you put the loaves in the oven, try not to bump or jar the loaves too much. Those air bubbles are a bit delicate, and you can make some strange-looking loaves if you cause the proofed dough to collapse.

At this point there should be enough activity left in your yeast to get what is called an "oven spring." This is a separation or splitting of the crust from the point where the pan and bread come together, either along the bottom of a round loaf or the level point in a loaf pan. If your oven spring is uneven (making your breads look like aliens), you haven't proofed the dough enough or the dough is too dry. If you don't have any spring, check the expiration date on your yeast.

Bake the loaves as directed in the recipe. Check for doneness by lifting the loaf and tapping it on the bottom; there should be a nice, hollow sound. The bread should have browned nicely. With more experience, you'll be able to tell from the evenness of the browning if the bread is finished.

Home ovens are remarkably inconsistent both in terms of temperature and heat distribution. Most of them have "hot" and "cold" spots and heat unevenly. To facilitate more even browning, rotate the pans halfway through the baking time. Bake some bread at the temperature suggested in the recipe, but you may need to set the temperature up or down, depending on the quirks of your particular oven. (An independent oven thermometer, available in housewares departments, would be a wise investment.)

You can tell that your oven is too hot if:

- You have small loaves, with no spring at all
- The outside looks done, but the inside is doughy or raw
- The loaves seem to be done before the time suggested in the recipe

You can tell that your oven is too cool if:

- The loaves are climbing out of the pan
- The crust is pale and the inside is dry
- The bread has been in the oven forever, and it still isn't done

Make notes in your cookbook after you've tried a recipe. Write down how long the loaves took to bake, what they looked like, and adjust the oven temperature accordingly next time you try the recipe.

Rotating the loaf halfway through the baking time can compensate for uneven heat circulation in your oven.

If your crust is too light or too dark, remember that the amount and type of sweetening affects the color. Check your measurements.

If your bread is splitting strangely, the dough was probably too dry. If your bread is flattening out, it was probably too wet.

Now, a word about dough, and you're ready to begin.

The "Good Dough"

IN MY RECIPES for yeasted breads, I refer to "a good dough." But what exactly does that mean? I keep coming back to an analogy: Making bread is kind of like raising a child. You don't really know if you've done a good job until the bread is out of the oven or the kid is out of your control.

Seriously, there are some general guidelines that you can use. But the best teacher will be your own experience.

If you're using white flour, a good dough is easy to recognize. It's smooth, elastic, and warm to the touch. There's an old baker's trick to determine when a dough like this is ready to be formed: hold a piece of the dough in both hands and stretch it until you can get a transparent center where you can see what is called the gluten film. If you're confident in the kitchen, you'll be able to recognize this stage after a couple of tries. If you're someone who is constantly second-guessing themselves, keep taking notes and comparing the feel of the dough and the finished product each time.

A dough that has been kneaded too long will begin to break down the gluten film and get sticky. A dough that has not been kneaded enough will be tough and break apart easily.

Recognizing when a whole-grain bread has gotten to the "good dough" stage is a little trickier. The bran in whole-grain breads acts like a little knife tearing at the attempt of the proteins to make a strong gluten film, so you need to recognize when to stop kneading by the stickiness of the dough rather than by appearance. Touch will tell you when the dough is no longer tacky, but you'll need to develop a frame of reference by comparing the finished products of a number of attempts.

Knowing when your dough has finished proofing (the last rise) is also something that comes with experience. The bread has finished rising when the surface is taut, or the dough has expanded to about twice its original size (unless a recipe specifies otherwise). You can tell if a bread has proofed too long if it comes out of the oven with an uneven, dimpled surface (kind of like a big chunk of cellulite). An underproofed loaf will have too much of an oven spring; that even tear along the edge of the pan that should be ¼ to ½ inch high.

In the bread-baking classes I've taught, I've noticed that the people who are most enamored with bread are the ones most intimidated by the thought of making it for themselves. The folks who really are just having some fun and looking forward to chowing down have a lot more success. Try to have a good time with this book. It's just a few cents' worth of ingredients, a few minutes of kneading, and some time with a good book while you're waiting for the dough to rise. And if it doesn't work this time, it'll be better the next time you try!

Daily Bread

I GREW UP ON the high plains of eastern Colorado, surrounded by expansive fields of grain and sugar beets. Every Friday, when the nine of us came home from school to face the obligatory Catholic lower-middle-class meal of tuna-noodle casserole or potato soup with homemade noodles or (aargh!) salmon patties fresh from the can, my mother always had a homemade, sweet-smelling apology ready for us—fresh, hot bread.

On those days when we were home for a snow day or in the early summer, my sisters and I would watch as she heated milk and butter, dissolved the yeast, and put together white bread to be baked in loaf pans, as dinner rolls and, best of all, cinnamon buns. Since there were so many of us, that meant six to eight loaves of bread and dozens of rolls and buns. But by Sunday after breakfast toast, we were back to the stuff that had been on sale in the grocery store that week—five loaves for a dollar.

I was first introduced to whole-grain breads and sourdough breads after I moved to Montana in 1977. A friend and neighbor who was also at home tending her babies gave me part of her sourdough starter. My first recipe and our own tradition began with sourdough bread twice a week, hot and covered with butter and homemade raspberry jam. It became my new family's comfort food, as my mother's home-baked breads had been mine. Montana wheat was considered the best—best-quality protein, best nutty taste, best folks doing the farming. The Mormon families kept bags and bags in their "emergency" stores, and their home mills ground the grains to produce their own versions of whole-grain breads.

So when my husband found himself without work and I was to be the income producer and he the chief caregiver, the transition to baking for a living was not that much of a stretch. Boston Daily Bread was started on a shoe-string budget, a wing and a prayer, and the everlasting hope that what we considered great bread in the mid- and far west would be accepted by tradition-bound New Englanders. We were right—good bread is good bread, no matter where you live.

In this book, we share the baking philosophy and many of the recipes (adapted for the home cook and home kitchen) that we use in our shops. Most of our breads and muffins have no added fats, oils, or preservatives and are made from all-natural ingredients. You'll get the very best taste and nutrition from these recipes if you can mill your own grain or use fresh, locally milled flour. However, having five children and a career or two, I know that *buying* bread, to say nothing of baking it, is enough of a labor of love without doing the Henny Penny thing and grinding your own grain. So all of the recipes in this book can be made with the flour you can find in any supermarket in the country, and they'll smell and taste delicious.

Do make sure your flour is fresh. I used to think that as long as flour didn't show signs of insect life it was fine, but old flour is best saved for papier mâché and homemade play dough.

As a professional baker, I buy almost every new bread book that comes on the market, and I laugh out loud when the first thing I read is "Twelve hours preparation time." My recipes won't keep you in the kitchen all day. While those Old World recipes make great breads, our New World lifestyle dictates that time be used differently. So the maximum rising time for these recipes is 2 hours, with another half hour or so to proof, or give the final rise to dough.

We'll start with white breads, the recipe my mother used and variations on that theme.

White Breads

*T*he breads in this chapter are "straight doughs." This means that all of the ingredients go into the first mixing. The dough rises and rests, then it is divided, proofed, and baked.

The standard rule in our shops is that if it has more white flour than whole-wheat flour, it's a straight dough.

These breads are very hearty and chewy. While you're mixing them, watch for a nice, smooth texture to develop as you have them "on the hook" in your mixer or in your hands as you knead.

Be creative: Substitute your favorite fruits or vegetables in these recipes, mixing in some herbs and spices to enhance the ingredients. Keep in mind that if the fruit or vegetable you're adding to a dough is acidic, be sure to add it at the end of the mix time, and be prepared to try your variation a couple of times to get it perfect.

You will notice that recipes with extra ingredients mention to "incorporate." This is usually language used for a muffin to keep it from toughening up, but in the breads, it means to get the "good dough" that we speak of, which is made by forming a good gluten film, and then adding the ingredient just until it is mixed through the dough. This is for two reasons. First, ingredients such as nuts or partially ground grains will cut through that gluten film and cause your dough to become sticky and lose elasticity. Secondly, herbs and more delicate ingredients (tomatoes or berries) will break up if mixed in at the beginning, graying the dough and losing that special individual flavor that comes from biting into a chunk of something.

Peasant White Bread

This white bread has no added fats or oils and a chewy, hearty texture. It's basically my mother's recipe, with the milk and butter she used removed. We sometimes call this bread Grandma's White Bread.

YIELD: TWO 1-POUND ROUNDS OR LOAVES

1½ cups warm water (95° to 100°F)
2 packages active dry yeast
3 cups unbleached all-purpose flour
¼ cup honey
1 tablespoon salt

Preheat the oven to 350 degrees. Spray two 9×5×3-inch loaf pans or a large cookie sheet.

In a small bowl, mix ½ cup of the water with the yeast until the yeast dissolves. *By hand:* Place the remaining water and the flour, honey, and salt in a large bowl. Add the yeast mixture and stir well, until a dough forms and pulls away from the sides of the bowl. Turn the dough onto a lightly floured surface and knead until you have a "good dough." *With a mixer:* Mix the dissolved yeast with the remaining water in the mixer bowl. Add 2½ cups of the flour, the honey, and the salt. Mix on low speed. Slowly add the last ½ cup flour to the bowl and continue mixing until the dough pulls away from the sides of the bowl. Turn the mixer to medium speed and continue mixing until a "good dough" forms. For both methods, proceed as below.

Place the dough back in the mixing bowl, cover with a damp towel, and let rise in a warm place for an hour. Punch the dough down, re-cover, and let rise for another hour.

Turn the dough out onto a floured work surface, divide into 2 equal pieces, and form into loaves of your desired shape. Place the loaves in the prepared pans or on the prepared cookie sheet and let rise, covered, in a warm place for 20 to 30 minutes.

Bake the loaves for 30 to 35 minutes. When the loaves are lightly browned, and sound hollow on the bottom when tapped, remove them from the oven. Remove them from the pans or cookie sheet to a wire rack to cool.

The loaves may be sliced when completely cooled. Tearing hot chunks off the cooling loaves is an acceptable alternative.

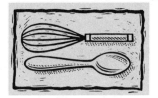

Jalapeño-Cheddar Bread

People who live in the Northeast have lots of fears—fear of crime, fear that their therapist will go away in August, fear of their children not being gifted—but their biggest fear is fear of hot peppers. It took a lot of cajoling to get our customers to try this bread, but now it's hard to keep up with the demand!

I think this bread is too special to use for sandwiches or as a vehicle for butter. Tear it into chunks to dip into soup or to eat alone.

YIELD: 2 LOAVES

1⅓ cups warm water (95 to 100°F)
2 packages active dry yeast
2¼ cups unbleached all-purpose flour
¾ cup coarsely ground yellow or white cornmeal
⅓ cup honey
1 tablespoon salt
¼ cup chopped jalapeño peppers
½ cup shredded sharp Cheddar cheese

Preheat the oven to 350°F. Spray two 9×5×3-inch loaf pans or a large cookie sheet.

In a small bowl, mix ⅓ cup of the water with the yeast until the yeast dissolves. *By hand:* Place the remaining water and the flour, cornmeal, honey, and salt in a large bowl. Add the yeast mixture and stir well, until a dough forms and pulls away from the sides of the bowl. Add the peppers and cheese and mix until incorporated. Turn the dough out onto a lightly floured work surface and knead until you have a "good dough." *With a mixer:* Mix the dissolved yeast with the remaining water in the mixer bowl. Add 1¾ cups of the flour, the cornmeal, the honey, and the salt. Mix on low speed. Slowly add the last ½ cup flour to the bowl and continue mixing until the dough pulls away from the sides of the bowl. Add the peppers and cheese and mix until they are incorporated into the dough. Turn the mixer to medium speed and continue mixing until a "good dough" forms. For both methods, proceed as below.

Place the dough back in the mixing bowl, cover with a damp towel, and let rise in a warm place for an hour. Punch the dough down, re-cover, and let rise for another hour.

Turn the dough out onto a floured work surface, divide into 2 equal pieces, and form into loaves of your desired shape. Place the loaves in the prepared pans or on the prepared cookie sheet and let rise, covered, in a warm place for 20 to 30 minutes.

Bake the loaves for 30 to 35 minutes. When the loaves are lightly browned, and sound hollow on the bottom when tapped, remove them from the oven. Remove the loaves from the pans or cookie sheet to a wire rack to cool.

Carrot-Tarragon Bread

This bread was designed to enhance chicken dishes—chicken soup, chicken salad, or chicken sandwiches—but it goes with a range of mild flavors. It's subtle but wonderfully soothing!

YIELD: 2 LOAVES

1½ cups warm water (95 to 100°F)
2 packages active dry yeast
3 cups unbleached all-purpose flour
¼ cup honey
1 tablespoon salt
1½ cups shredded carrots
2 tablespoons finely chopped fresh tarragon or 2 teaspoons dried

Preheat the oven to 350°F. Spray two 9×5×3-inch loaf pans or a large cookie sheet.

In a small bowl, mix ½ cup of the water with the yeast until the yeast dissolves. *By hand:* Place the remaining water, flour, honey, and salt in a large bowl. Add the yeast mixture and stir well, until a dough forms and pulls away from the sides of the bowl. Add the carrots and tarragon and mix until they are incorporated. Turn the dough out onto a lightly floured surface and knead until you have a "good dough." *With a mixer:* Mix the dissolved yeast with the remaining water in the mixer bowl. Add 2½ cups of the flour, the honey, and the salt. Mix on low speed. Slowly add the last ½ cup flour to the bowl and continue mixing until the dough pulls away from the sides of the bowl. Add the carrots and tarragon and mix until they are just incorporated. Turn the mixer to medium speed and continue mixing until a "good dough" forms. For both methods, proceed as below.

Place the dough back in the mixing bowl, cover with a damp towel, and let rise in a warm place for an hour. Punch the dough down, re-cover, and let rise for another hour.

Turn the dough out onto a floured work surface, divide into 2 equal pieces, and form into loaves of your desired shape. Place the loaves in the prepared pans or on the prepared cookie sheet and let rise, covered, in a warm place for 20 to 30 minutes.

Bake the loaves for 30 to 35 minutes. When the loaves are lightly browned, and sound hollow on the bottom when tapped, remove them from the oven. Remove the loaves from the pans or cookie sheet to a wire rack to cool completely.

Sun-Dried Tomato and Olive Bread

I have very specific ideas (and tastes) about what are summer foods and what are winter foods. I put this bread in the summer foods category, but you can make this bread anytime and have a taste of summer all year round. I like this bread with a little cheese, a little wine, and a lot of sunshine.

YIELD: 2 LOAVES

1½ cups warm water (95 to 100°F)
2 packages active dry yeast
3 cups unbleached all-purpose flour
¼ cup honey
1 tablespoon salt
1 cup chopped sun-dried tomatoes, soaked for 30 minutes, drained, and patted dry
½ cup chopped, pitted Kalamata olives

Preheat the oven to 350°F. Spray two 9×5×3-inch loaf pans or a large cookie sheet.

In a small bowl, mix ½ cup of the water with the yeast until the yeast dissolves. *By hand:* Place the remaining water, flour, honey, and salt in a large bowl. Add the yeast mixture and stir well, until a dough forms and pulls away from the sides of the bowl. Add the sun-dried tomatoes and olives and mix until they are incorporated. Turn the dough out onto a lightly floured work surface and knead until you have a "good dough." *With a mixer:* Mix the dissolved yeast with the remaining water in the mixer bowl. Add 2½ cups of the flour, the honey, and the salt. Mix on low speed. Slowly add the last ½ cup flour to the bowl and continue mixing until the dough pulls away from the sides of the bowl. Add the sun-dried tomatoes and olives and mix until they are just incorporated. Turn the mixer to medium speed and continue mixing until a "good dough" forms. For both methods, proceed as below.

Place the dough back in the mixing bowl, cover with a damp towel, and let rise in a warm place for an hour. Punch the dough down, re-cover, and let rise for another hour.

Turn the dough out onto a floured surface, divide into 2 equal pieces, and form into loaves of your desired shape. Place the loaves in the prepared pans or on the prepared cookie sheet and let rise, covered, in a warm place for 20 to 30 minutes.

Bake the loaves for 30 to 35 minutes. When the loaves are lightly browned, and sound hollow on the bottom when tapped, remove them from the oven. Remove the loaves from the pans or cookie sheet to a wire rack to cool.

Cinnamon, Apple, and Raisin Loaf

This bread is great in the morning toasted and slathered with cream cheese. You can use dried apples if you soak them for about half an hour and dry them well before you add them to the dough.

YIELD: 2 LOAVES

1½ cups warm water (95 to 100°F)
2 packages active dry yeast
3 cups unbleached all-purpose flour
¼ cup honey
1 tablespoon salt
1 cup finely chopped, peeled apples
2 teaspoons ground cinnamon
½ cup dark raisins

Preheat the oven to 350°F. Spray two 9×5×3-inch loaf pans or a large cookie sheet.

In a small bowl, mix ½ cup of the water with the yeast until the yeast dissolves. *By hand:* Place the remaining water, flour, honey, and salt in a large bowl. Add the yeast mixture and stir well, until a dough forms and pulls away from the sides of the bowl. Add the apples, cinnamon, and raisins and mix until they are incorporated. Turn the dough out onto a lightly floured work surface and knead until you have a "good dough." *With a mixer:* Mix the dissolved yeast with the remaining water in the mixer bowl. Add 2½ cups of the flour, the honey, and the salt. Mix on low speed. Slowly add the last ½ cup flour to the bowl and continue mixing until the dough pulls away from the sides of the bowl. Add the apples, cinnamon, and raisins and mix until they are just incorporated. Turn the mixer to medium speed and continue mixing until a "good dough" forms. For both methods, proceed as below.

Place the dough back in the mixing bowl, cover with a damp towel, and let rise in a warm place for an hour. Punch the dough down, re-cover, and let rise for another hour.

Turn the dough out onto a floured surface, divide into 2 equal pieces, and form into loaves of your desired shape. Place the loaves in the prepared pans or on the prepared cookie sheet and let rise, covered, in a warm place for 20 to 30 minutes.

Bake the loaves for 30 to 35 minutes. When the loaves are lightly browned, and sound hollow on the bottom when tapped, remove them from the oven. Remove the loaves from the pans or cookie sheet to a wire rack to cool.

Anadama Bread

Anadama bread is a yummy corn and molasses loaf that many native New Englanders remember from their childhoods. There are lots of stories and theories about the origins of this loaf, but the most plausible seems to be that as different grains were unavailable, corn and wheat would be mixed to create this yeasted loaf. Molasses was a New England staple.

This dough will clean the bowl but will not be very stiff. The cornmeal leaves the dough a little slack, but it should not be sticky.

YIELD: 2 LOAVES

1⅓ cups warm water (95 to 100°F)
2 packages active dry yeast
2¼ cups unbleached all-purpose flour
¾ cup coarsely ground yellow or white cornmeal
⅓ cup honey
1 tablespoon salt

Preheat the oven to 350°F. Spray two 9×5×3-inch loaf pans or a large cookie sheet.

In a small bowl, mix ⅓ cup of the water with the yeast until the yeast dissolves. *By hand:* Place the remaining water, flour, cornmeal, honey, and salt in a large bowl. Add the yeast mixture and stir well, until a dough forms and pulls away from the sides of the bowl. Turn the dough out onto a lightly floured work surface and knead until you have a "good dough." *With a mixer:* Mix the dissolved yeast with the remaining water in the mixer bowl. Add 2½ cups of the flour, the cornmeal, the honey, and the salt. Mix on low speed. Slowly add the last ½ cup flour to the bowl and continue mixing until the dough pulls away from the sides of the bowl. Turn the mixer to medium speed and continue mixing until a "good dough" forms. For both methods, proceed as below.

Place the dough back in the mixing bowl, cover with a damp towel, and let rise in a warm place for an hour. Punch the dough down, re-cover, and let rise for another hour.

Turn the dough out onto a floured surface, divide into 2 equal pieces, and form into loaves of your desired shape. Place the loaves in the prepared pans or on the prepared cookie sheet and let rise, covered, in a warm place for 20 to 30 minutes.

Bake the loaves for 30 to 35 minutes. When the loaves are lightly browned, remove them from the oven. Remove the loaves from the pans or cookie sheet to a wire rack to cool.

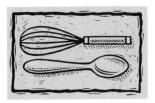

Cinnamon Swirl Bread

This is an adaptation of our ever-popular, slightly decadent cinnamon swirl loaf. We make two or three batches of seventy-eight loaves by hand every day, but this recipe has been scaled down to make two loaves. They won't last long!

YIELD: 2 LOAVES

DOUGH:

1½ cups warm water (95 to 100°F)
2 packages active dry yeast
3¼ cups unbleached all-purpose flour
¼ cup honey
1 tablespoon salt

FILLING:

¾ cup honey
¼ cup ground cinnamon

Preheat the oven to 350°F. Spray two 9×5×3-inch loaf pans.

In a small bowl, mix ½ cup of the water with the yeast until the yeast dissolves. *By hand:* Place the remaining water, 2½ cups flour, honey, and salt in a large bowl. Add the yeast mixture and stir well, until a dough forms and pulls away from the sides of the bowl. Add the last ½ cup of flour and continue mixing. This dough should be a little dry. Turn the dough out onto a lightly floured work surface and knead until you have a "good dough." *With a mixer:* Mix the dissolved yeast with the remaining water in the mixer bowl. Add 2½ cups of the flour, the honey, and the salt. Mix on low speed. Slowly add the last ½ cup flour to the bowl and continue mixing until the dough pulls away from the sides of the bowl. Turn the mixer to medium speed and continue mixing until a "good dough" forms. For both methods, proceed as below.

Place the dough back in the mixing bowl. Mix together the ¾ cup honey and cinnamon. Pour this mixture over the dough, cover with a damp towel, and let rise in a warm place for an hour. Punch the dough down gently, only to deflate it; do not mix the honey-cinnamon mixture into the dough. Re-cover the dough and let rise for another hour.

Lift the dough carefully onto a very well floured surface so the dry side is down and divide it into 2 equal pieces. Without disturbing the honey-cinnamon mixture, roll up each piece of dough so the honey-cinnamon mixture is in the center, pushing as much air out of the dough as possible. Place the loaves, seam side down, in the prepared pans and let rise, covered, in a warm place for 20 to 30 minutes

Bake the loaves for 30 to 35 minutes. When the loaves are lightly browned, and sound hollow on the bottom when tapped, remove them from the oven. Remove the loaves from the pans to a wire rack to cool.

Focaccia

Focaccia is a fairly recent addition to the Daily Bread roster. We introduced it in our stores at the suggestion of Dave McClean and David Deal from the Stone Mill Bread Store in Winston-Salem, North Carolina. It was an instant hit!

My favorite topping is potato, sun-dried tomato, rosemary, and kosher salt, but this bread is a perfect canvas for your creativity or any leftovers in cupboard or fridge. These are equally good hot or cold, making them perfect picnic, snack, or lunchbox treats.

YIELD: 4 FOCACCIAS

DOUGH:

2 packages active dry yeast
2½ cups warm water (90 to 110°F)
4¾ cups unbleached all-purpose flour
½ teaspoon salt
¼ cup olive or vegetable oil

TOPPING:

¼ cup olive oil
I teaspoon kosher salt
¼ teaspoon coarsely ground black pepper
I teaspoon fresh rosemary, oregano, sage, or marjoram leaves, or a combination of these
½ cup dry-pack sun-dried tomatoes, soaked for 20 minutes in hot water and drained
I cup thinly sliced, peeled potato

Cornmeal for cookie sheets

Preheat the oven to 450°F. Sprinkle 2 cookie sheets liberally with cornmeal.
In a small bowl, dissolve the yeast in the water. Mix the flour and salt in a

large bowl and make a well. Pour in the oil and the yeast mixture and mix, either by hand or with a mixer, until a ball forms. Cover the dough with a damp towel and let it rest for 30 minutes.

By hand: Turn the dough out onto a lightly floured surface and knead for 8 to 10 minutes, or until the dough is smooth and satiny to the touch. Put the dough back into the bowl. *With a mixer:* Mix at medium speed until the dough is smooth and satiny to the touch, about, 6 to 7 minutes. For both methods, proceed with the recipe below.

Cover the dough and let rise 1 to 2 hours, or until doubled in size. Punch the dough down and turn it out. Divide the dough into 4 equal pieces and shape each piece into a flat round. Prick each round with a fork several times. Brush with olive oil, then sprinkle with the salt, pepper, and herbs and top with the tomatoes and potatoes.

Let rise for approximately 30 minutes. Bake at 450°F for 20 minutes, then reduce the oven temperature to 350°F and bake for another 20 minutes. Remove from the cookie sheets and cool on wire racks.

Challah

This is a rich, buttery braided bread. We make it plain or with golden raisins, glazed with an egg wash and sprinkled with poppy or sesame seeds.

YIELD: 2 LOAVES

DOUGH:

2½ cups very warm water (110 to 115°F)
2 packages active dry yeast
6 cups unbleached all-purpose flour
1½ cups whole-wheat flour
½ cup butter, very soft but not melted
½ cup sugar
1½ tablespoons salt
2 large eggs, at room temperature

EGG WASH:

1 large egg, well beaten
¼ cup water

Sesame or poppy seeds, for garnish

Preheat the oven to 350°F. Spray a large cookie sheet.

In a small bowl, mix ½ cup of the water with the yeast until the yeast dissolves. In a large bowl, combine the all-purpose and whole-wheat flours.

In another large bowl, mix 4 cups of the flour mixture with the remaining water, butter, sugar, salt, and eggs. *By hand:* Mix thoroughly, and add the yeast mixture. Continue to mix, adding the remaining flour mixture until a dough forms and pulls away from the side of the bowl. This should take approximately 10 minutes. *With a mixer:* Add the yeast mixture to the flours, the remaining water, butter, sugar, salt and eggs. Mix for 1 minute at low speed. Add the remaining flour mixture and continue mixing at medium speed for about 5 minutes, until a dough forms and pulls away from the sides of the bowl. For both methods, proceed as below.

Turn the dough out onto a lightly floured work surface and knead for 5 to 8 minutes, adding more flour if necessary. Place the dough in a bowl, cover with a damp towel, and let rise in a warm place for about 90 minutes or until doubled in size.

Punch the dough down, turn it out onto the work surface, cut it in half. Divide each half into 3 equal pieces, and roll each piece into a strand 10 to 12 inches long.

Squeeze the ends of three strands together, and tuck them under. Braid the strands, and when you reach the opposite ends, squeeze them together and tuck them under. Repeat with the remaining strands of dough.

Place the loaves on the prepared cookie sheet. Cover and let rise in a warm place for approximately 1 hour.

Mix the beaten egg with the water, and using a pastry brush, coat the top of the loaves with the mixture. Sprinkle with sesame or poppy seeds.

Bake for 30 to 35 minutes. When the loaves are golden brown and sound hollow on the bottom when tapped, remove them from the oven. Remove the loaves from the cookie sheet to a wire rack to cool.

Apple-Cinnamon Swirl Bread

My wonderful, talented, bossy manager, Diane Siniawski, first experimented with this recipe in the fall of 1995. I was skeptical about how well it would sell until we started getting orders for it from all over the state.

You can use dried apples, canned sliced apples, or if you have the time, freshly peeled and sliced Granny Smith apples.

YIELD: 2 LOAVES

DOUGH:

1½ cups warm water (95 to 100°F)
2 packages active dry yeast
3¼ cups unbleached all-purpose flour
¼ cup honey
1 tablespoon salt

FILLING:

1 cup sliced apples, dried, canned and drained, or peeled, fresh
1 cup honey
¼ cup ground cinnamon

GLAZE (OPTIONAL):

¼ cup honey
1 tablespoon ground cinnamon

Preheat the oven to 350°F. Spray two 9×5×3-inch loaf pans.

In a small bowl, mix ½ cup of the water with the yeast until the yeast dissolves. *By hand:* Place the remaining water, 2½ cups flour, honey, and salt in a large bowl. Add the yeast mixture and stir well, until a dough forms and pulls away from the sides of the bowl. Add the last ½ cup flour and continue mixing. This dough should be a little dry. Turn the dough out onto a lightly floured work surface and knead until you have a "good dough." *With a mixer:* Mix the dissolved yeast with the remaining water in the mixer bowl. Add 2½ cups of the flour, the honey, and the salt. Mix on low speed. Slowly add the last ½ cup flour to the bowl and continue mixing until the dough pulls away from the sides of the bowl. Turn the mixer to medium speed and continue mixing until a "good dough" forms. For both methods, proceed as below.

Place the dough back in the mixing bowl, cover with a damp towel, and let rise in a warm place for an hour. Punch the dough down, re-cover, and let rise for another hour.

While the dough rises, mix in a small bowl the apples, honey, and cinnamon for the filling.

Turn the dough out onto a floured work surface, and divide into 2 equal pieces. Roll each piece into a 12-by-8-inch rectangle. Spread half of the apple, honey, and cinnamon mixture on each rectangle and knead it into the dough slightly. Roll the dough up like a jelly roll and place, seam side down, in the prepared pans. Let rise, covered, in a warm place for 20 to 30 minutes.

Bake for 30 to 35 minutes. When the loaves are lightly browned, and sound hollow on the bottom when tapped, remove them from the oven. Turn the loaves out of the pans onto a wire rack. Be careful you don't burn yourself on the apple, honey, and cinnamon mixture; it stays hotter than the bread.

Let the loaves cool for 10 minutes. Mix the remaining honey and cinnamon together and brush over the top of the loaves. Let cool completely.

Outrageous Rye Bread

It's hard to make a great loaf using only rye flour. We combine white, whole wheat, and rye flours to make the Outrageous Rye Bread for our stores; this adaptation uses white and rye. Don't be put off by the sauerkraut—it adds moisture and a tangy flavor.

YIELD: 2 LOAVES

I cup warm water (105 to 110°F)
2 packages active dry yeast
6 cups unbleached all-purpose flour
2 cups rye flour
¼ cup caraway seeds
I cup drained sauerkraut

Preheat the oven to 350°F. Spray two 9×5×3-inch loaf pans or a large cookie sheet.

In a large bowl, combine the all-purpose flour and rye flour. Mix ¼ cup of the water with the yeast until the yeast dissolves. *By hand:* Place the remaining water, the flours, caraway seeds, and sauerkraut in a large bowl. Add the yeast mixture and stir well, until a dough forms and pulls away from the sides of the bowl. Turn the dough out onto a lightly floured work surface and knead until you have a "good dough." Rye flour makes a sticky dough, so don't expect the same satiny texture you get with a well-kneaded white flour dough. *With a mixer:* Mix the dissolved yeast with the remaining water in the mixer bowl. Add 7½ cups of the flour, the honey, and the salt. Mix on low speed. Add the caraway seeds and sauerkraut. Slowly add the last ½ cup flour to the bowl and continue mixing until the dough pulls away from the sides of the bowl. Turn the mixer to medium speed and continue mixing until a "good dough" forms. For both methods, proceed as below.

Place the dough back in the mixing bowl, cover with a damp towel, and let rise in a warm place for an hour. Punch the dough down, re-cover, and let rise for another hour.

Turn the dough out onto a floured work surface, divide into 2 equal pieces, and form into loaves of your desired shape. Place the loaves in the prepared pans or on the prepared cookie sheet and let rise, covered, in a warm place for 20 to 30 minutes.

Brush or spray the loaves with water and bake for 35 to 40 minutes. When the loaves sound hollow on the bottom when tapped, remove them from the oven. Remove the loaves from the pans or cookie sheet to a wire rack to cool.

Whole-Wheat Breads

When we started the first Boston Daily Bread, we were starting over. Scott was forty-one and I was thirty-six. We thought we had settled in for the long haul in Colorado, but life doesn't always work like that.

When we made the decision to open a bakery, it was not only the 2,000-plus-mile move, it was truly purging ourselves of our old life. We were starting from scratch. Our home and most of our possessions were sold. We cashed in all the retirement money we had, the kids' savings bonds and savings accounts and college money.

During this transition, the meaning of "home" changed radically. For most Americans "home" means property. But when your home has been taken from you by divorce, the loss of a job, or a catastrophe, the word "home" takes on a whole new meaning. "Home" is the means by which you are protected. It is the space you share as a family. Our new home had to be made in someone else's house; we made that safe space by bringing our special family customs and traditions into that space. Baking bread, one of the most basic ways of providing love and nurture, was the key to creating our new home.

Three years later, we have lived in three different shelters, and our attitudes about what is "home" are far more flexible. We all understand that we don't own homes, they own us. We borrow our space for as long as we are meant to be there and then move on, whether across the street, the continent, the world, or on to the next world. Making this space "home" is all about things like love, laughter, and the goodness of home-made bread.

Honey Whole-Wheat Bread

The surge in growth in whole-grain bakeries is a direct result, in my opinion, of the rediscovery of the heavenly taste of bread baked from fresh-milled flour.

Honey Whole-Wheat is the mainstay of our whole-grain breads. It is the "mother bread" from which all the rest come. This bread is made with a "sponge," a wet mixture of yeast, water, honey, and flour that is allowed to stand for a couple of hours and gives the heavy whole-wheat dough an extra boost in rising. We've modified the recipe to accommodate the use of store-bought flour, but this is still one of the best breads you'll ever taste.

YIELD: 2 LOAVES

SPONGE:

1¼ cups warm water (about 105°F)
2 packages active dry yeast
½ cup honey
1½ cups whole-wheat flour

DOUGH:

1¼ cups warm water (95 to 100°F)
1 package active dry yeast
3 cups whole-wheat flour
1 tablespoon salt

Make the sponge: In a large bowl, mix the water with the yeast until the yeast dissolves. Add the honey and flour and mix until combined. Cover with a damp towel and let sit in a warm place for 2 hours.

Preheat the oven to 350°F. Spray two 9×5×3-inch loaf pans or a large cookie sheet.

Make the dough: In a small bowl, mix ¼ cup of the water with the yeast until the yeast dissolves. *By hand:* Stir down the sponge. Add the remaining water, the flour, and the salt, then add the yeast mixture and stir well, until a dough forms and pulls away from the sides of the bowl. Turn the dough out onto a lightly floured work surface and knead until you have a "good dough," about 3 to 5 minutes. The dough will remain a bit sticky. *With a mixer:* In the mixer bowl, combine the yeast mixture with the rest of the water. Add 2½ cups of the flour, the salt, and sponge mixture. Mix on low speed. Slowly add the last ½ cup flour to the bowl and continue mixing until the dough pulls away from the sides of the bowl. Turn the mixer to medium and continue mixing until a "good dough" forms. For both methods, proceed as below.

Let the dough rest for 5 minutes, then divide into 2 equal parts and shape into loaves of your desired shape. Place in prepared pans or on the prepared cookie sheet, and let rise, covered, in a warm place, until doubled in size, about 30 minutes.

Bake the loaves for 30 to 40 minutes. When the loaves are lightly browned, and sound hollow on the bottom when tapped, remove them from the oven. Remove them from the pans or cookie sheet to a wire rack to cool.

Mushroom, Parsley, and Jack Cheese Whole-Wheat Bread

I love texture in my food, and this bread fills the bill. The crunchy parsley, moist mushrooms, and chewy cheese make this interesting to the last bite

You must make this bread with fresh parsley. You can, however, use any mushroom that appeals to you. If you want to use canned mushrooms, reduce the water in the sponge to 1 cup. Low-fat or fat-free jack cheese can be used.

YIELD: 2 LOAVES

SPONGE:

1¼ cups warm water (about 105°F)
2 packages active dry yeast
½ cup honey
1½ cups whole-wheat flour
1 cup chopped fresh parsley

DOUGH:

1¼ cups warm water (95 to 100°F)
1 package active dry yeast
3 cups whole-wheat flour
1 tablespoon salt
1 cup coarsely chopped mushrooms
½ cup shredded Monterey Jack cheese
2 cubes (1 inch each) Monterey Jack cheese, for garnish

Make the sponge: In a large bowl, mix the water with the yeast until the yeast dissolves. Add the honey, flour, and parsley and mix until combined. Cover with a damp towel and let sit in a warm place for 2 hours.

Preheat the oven to 350°F. Spray two 9×5×3-inch loaf pans or a large cookie sheet.

Make the dough: In a small bowl, mix ¼ cup of the water with the yeast until the yeast dissolves. *By hand:* Stir down the sponge. Add the remaining water, the flour, salt, and mushrooms, then the yeast mixture and stir well, until a dough forms and pulls away from the sides of the bowl. Turn the dough out onto a lightly floured work surface and knead until you have a "good dough," about 3 to 5 minutes. Knead in the cheese. The dough will remain a bit sticky. *With a mixer:* In the mixer bowl, combine the yeast with the rest of the water. Add 2½ cups of the flour, the salt, mushrooms, and sponge mixture. Mix on low speed. Slowly add the last ½ cup flour to the bowl and continue mixing until the dough pulls away from the sides of the bowl. Turn the mixer to medium and continue mixing until a "good dough" forms. Mix in the cheese until just combined. For both methods, proceed as below.

Let the dough rest for 5 minutes, then divide into 2 equal pieces and shape into loaves of your desired shape. Garnish each loaf with a cube of cheese. Place in the prepared pans or on the prepared cookie sheet, and let rise, covered, in a warm place, until doubled in size, about 30 minutes.

Bake the loaves for 30 to 40 minutes. When the loaves are lightly browned, and sound hollow on the bottom when tapped, remove them from the oven. Remove the loaves from the pans or cookie sheet to a wire rack to cool.

Swiss and Spinach Whole-Wheat Bread

This is a pretty bread to look at, with a "complete sandwich" taste. The stronger flavor the cheese has, the better. If you're using fresh spinach, make sure you get all the grit and dirt out of the leaves. If you use a low-fat Swiss, the texture of the bread will be firmer.

YIELD: 2 LOAVES

SPONGE:

1¼ cups warm water (about 105°F)
2 packages active dry yeast
½ cup honey
1½ cups whole-wheat flour
1 cup (firmly packed) chopped, well-washed spinach

DOUGH:

1¼ cups warm water (95 to 100°F)
1 package active dry yeast
3 cups whole-wheat flour
1 tablespoon salt
½ cup shredded Swiss cheese

Make the sponge: In a large bowl, mix the water with the yeast until the yeast dissolves. Add the honey, flour, and spinach and mix until combined. Cover with a damp towel and let sit in a warm place for 2 hours.

Preheat the oven to 350°F. Spray two 9×5×3-inch loaf pans or a large cookie sheet.

Make the dough: In a small bowl, mix the yeast with ¼ cup of the water until the yeast dissolves. *By hand:* Stir down the sponge. Add the remaining water, the flour, and the salt, then add the yeast mixture and stir well, until a dough forms and pulls away from the sides of the bowl. Turn the dough out onto a lightly floured work surface and knead until you have a "good dough," about 3 to 5 minutes. Knead in the cheese. The dough will remain a bit sticky. *With a mixer:* In the mixer bowl, combine the yeast mixture with the rest of the water. Add 2½ cups of the flour, the salt, and sponge mixture. Mix on low speed. Slowly add the last ½ cup flour to the bowl and continue mixing until the dough pulls away from the sides of the bowl. Turn the mixer to medium and continue mixing until a "good dough" forms. Mix in the cheese until just combined. For both methods, proceed as below.

Let the dough rest for 5 minutes, then divide into 2 equal parts and shape into 2 loaves of your desired shape. Place in the prepared pans or on the prepared cookie sheet, and let rise, covered, in a warm place, until doubled in size.

Bake the loaves for 30 to 40 minutes. When the loaves are lightly browned, and sound hollow on the bottom when tapped, remove them from the oven. Remove the loaves from the pans or cookie sheet to a wire rack to cool.

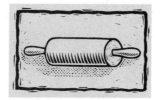

Carrot-Orange Whole-Wheat Bread

The nutty taste of whole wheat mixes beautifully with the crunchy carrots and flavor of orange in this hearty loaf. It makes terrific turkey sandwiches.

If you can find orange oil (not extract!), it adds a delicious extra dimension to this bread. Use no more than ½ teaspoon, and add it to the dough ingredients. You can find orange oil at gourmet stores and some well-stocked supermarkets.

YIELD: 2 LOAVES

SPONGE:

1¼ cups warm water (about 105°F)
2 packages active dry yeast
½ cup honey
1½ cups whole-wheat flour

DOUGH:

1¼ cups warm water (95 to 100°F)
1 package active dry yeast
3 cups whole-wheat flour
1 tablespoon salt
2 tablespoons grated orange peel
1 cup grated carrots

Make the sponge: In a large bowl, mix the water with the yeast until the yeast dissolves. Add the honey and flour and mix until combined. Cover with a damp towel and let sit in a warm place for 2 hours.

Preheat the oven to 350°F. Spray two 9×5×3-inch loaf pans or a large cookie sheet.

Make the dough: In a small bowl, mix ¼ cup of the water with the yeast until the yeast dissolves. *By hand:* Stir down the sponge. Add the remaining water, the flour, salt, orange peel, and carrots, then add the yeast mixture and stir well, until a dough forms and pulls away from the sides of the bowl. Turn the dough out onto a lightly floured work surface and knead until you have a "good dough," about 3 to 5 minutes. The dough will remain a bit sticky. *With a mixer:* In the mixer bowl, combine the yeast mixture with the rest of the water. Add 2½ cups of the flour, the salt, orange peel, carrots, and sponge mixture. Mix on low speed. Slowly add the last ½ cup flour to the bowl and continue mixing until the dough pulls away from the sides of the bowl. Turn the mixer to medium and continue mixing until a "good dough" forms. For both methods, proceed as below.

Let the dough rest for 5 minutes, then shape into 2 loaves. Place in the prepared pans or on the prepared cookie sheet, and let rise, covered, in a warm place, until doubled in size.

Bake the loaves for 30 to 40 minutes. When the loaves are lightly browned, and sound hollow on the bottom when tapped, remove them from the oven. Remove the loaves from the pans or cookie sheet to a wire rack to cool.

Cherry, Walnut, and Vanilla Whole-Wheat Bread

These are three of my family's favorite flavors, all rolled up into one bread. It's a terrific breakfast, snack, or teatime treat. Make your walnut pieces big and halve the cherries to give this sweet bread extra texture. Adding more vanilla will make the bread an unappetizing color, so if the vanilla flavor isn't strong enough for you, try glazing the cooled loaves with a mixture of confectioners' sugar, milk, and vanilla.

YIELD: 2 LOAVES

SPONGE:

1¼ cups warm water (about 105°F)
2 packages active dry yeast
½ cup honey
1½ cups whole-wheat flour

DOUGH:

1 package active dry yeast
1¼ cups warm water (95 to 100°F)
2 tablespoons vanilla
3 cups whole-wheat flour
1 tablespoon salt
½ cup halved dried sweet cherries
½ cup coarsely chopped walnuts

Make the sponge: In a large bowl, mix the water with the yeast until the yeast dissolves. Add the honey and flour and mix until combined. Cover with a damp towel and let sit in a warm place for 2 hours.

Preheat the oven to 350°F. Spray two 9×5×3-inch loaf pans or a large cookie sheet.

Make the dough: In a small bowl, mix ¼ cup of the water with the yeast until the yeast dissolves. *By hand:* Stir down the sponge. Add the remaining water, the vanilla, the flour, and the salt, then add the yeast mixture and stir well, until a dough forms and pulls away from the sides of the bowl. Turn the dough out onto a lightly floured work surface and knead until you have a "good dough," about 3 to 5 minutes. Add the cherries and walnuts and knead them into the dough. The dough will remain a bit sticky. *With a mixer:* In the mixer bowl, combine the yeast mixture with the rest of the water. Add 2½ cups of the flour, the salt, and sponge mixture. Mix on low speed. Slowly add the last ½ cup flour to the bowl and continue mixing until the dough pulls away from the sides of the bowl. Turn the mixer to medium and continue mixing until a "good dough" forms. Add the cherries and walnuts and mix until just combined. For both methods, proceed as below.

Let the dough rest for 5 minutes, then divide into 2 equal pieces and shape into loaves of your desired shape. Place in the prepared pans or on the prepared cookie sheet, and let rise, covered, in a warm place, until doubled in size.

Bake the loaves for 30 to 40 minutes. When the loaves are lightly browned, and sound hollow on the bottom when tapped, remove them from the oven. Remove the loaves from the pans or cookie sheet to a wire rack to cool.

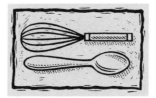

Honey-Oat Whole-Wheat Bread

Here's a delicious way to get the health benefits of oats. This bread needs a little bit of oil to compensate for the amount of liquid absorbed by the oats. Use canola oil or a very, very mild extra-virgin olive oil. Do not use quick or instant oats in this recipe; they will collapse into the dough.

YIELD: 2 LOAVES

SPONGE:

1¼ cups warm water (about 105°F)
2 packages active dry yeast
½ cup honey
1½ cups whole-wheat flour
½ cup rolled oats
¼ cup canola oil

DOUGH:

1¼ cups warm water (95 to 100°F)
1 package active dry yeast
3 cups whole-wheat flour
1 tablespoon salt

Make the sponge: In a large bowl, mix the water with the yeast until the yeast dissolves. Add the honey, flour, oats, and oil and mix until combined. Cover with a damp towel and let sit in a warm place for 2 hours.

Preheat the oven to 350°F. Spray two 9×5×3-inch loaf pans or a large cookie sheet.

Make the dough: In a small bowl, mix ¼ cup of the water with the yeast until the yeast dissolves. *By hand:* Stir down the sponge. Add the remaining water, the flour, and the salt, then add the yeast mixture and stir well, until a dough forms and pulls away from the sides of the bowl. Turn the dough out onto a lightly floured work surface and knead until you have a "good dough," about 3 to 5 minutes. The dough will remain a bit sticky. *With a mixer:* In the mixer bowl, combine the yeast mixture with the rest of the water. Add 2½ cups of the flour, the salt, and sponge mixture. Mix on low speed. Slowly add the last ½ cup flour to the bowl and continue mixing until the dough pulls away from the sides of the bowl. Turn the mixer to medium and continue mixing until a "good dough" forms. For both methods, proceed as below.

Let the dough rest for 5 minutes, then shape into 2 loaves. Place in the prepared pans or on the prepared cookie sheet, and let rise, covered, in a warm place, until doubled in size.

Bake the loaves for 30 to 40 minutes. When the loaves are lightly browned, and sound hollow on the bottom when tapped, remove them from the oven. Remove the loaves from the pans or cookie sheet to a wire rack to cool.

Bread Machines

*F*rankly, writing this chapter was like going in for a root canal. I have been suspicious of these creatures since they first appeared in the mass market, perhaps because they became popular at the same time my first store was really taking off!

I have yet to have a loaf of yeasted bread from a machine that I consider real bread. Bread-machine bread is to real bread what Velveeta is to real cheese.

When I purchased a machine to create these recipes, I bought a West Bend for purely emotional reasons: the new model had a real-looking bread pan that formed a true loaf-sized and -shaped bread. But when I looked at the pictures of the bread on the box and the book of instructions, I wondered: Why are the tops bumpy and uneven? Why do the loaves collapse during the baking cycle? If I tried to sell bread that looked like this, I'd be in big trouble!

It was just as I'd always suspected: these machines were nothing but expensive room deodorizers; they sell convenience and smell at the expense of taste and texture.

I had my kids use the machine to make bread; it was an easy project for them. When they tasted the results, they said they would be happy to have gone to the bakery to help out instead.

But if you've made the investment, and saving time is a serious consideration, let me show you how to get the best bread possible out of your machines.

- **Eliminate the dried milk.** It's in almost all bread machine recipes, and the closed environment of the bread machine creates a taste that is overpowering.

- **Substitute oil for butter or margarine.** Without the fat, bread machine breads are simply too tough to eat cool. A light olive oil is a healthier alternative to the butter and margarine usually called for in bread machine recipes.

- **If you use fresh yeast, use 40 percent less than the amount of dried yeast called for in the recipe.** Make sure your measurements are precise.

- **Use the extended-rise setting for all whole-grain breads.** It will give the bread more volume.

- **Replace sugar with honey.** Use half the amount of honey as the amount of sugar called for in the recipe.

- **Hand-knead before the last rise cycle.** If you're around, you can open the machine as it starts the last rise cycle and hand shape the loaf. This will even out the top and make it look like real bread—if you don't turn it over and look at the holes in the bottom!

Most of the recipes in the "White Breads" section of this book can be adapted for your bread machine. If there are additions to the dough, such as cheese, nuts, fruits, or vegetables, add them at the "nuts and fruits" point of the cycle. If you have an extended-rise option, use it.

Do not attempt to use any of the recipes that require a sponge.

Country White

This chewy bread has a nice flavor, but a loose crumb—I wouldn't use it for sandwiches. It's fine with butter and jam or as a "tear apart" with soup. You can also use this dough to make filled "pockets" for lunches or snacks, or quick cinnamon rolls.

YIELD: ONE 2-POUND LOAF

1½ cups skim milk
2 tablespoons extra-virgin olive oil
4 cups unbleached all-purpose flour
1 tablespoon honey
1½ teaspoons salt
1 package active dry yeast

Carefully measure all the ingredients into the bread-machine pan, and follow the manufacturer's instructions. Do not use the extended-rise cycle for this bread, but do use the "dark crust" setting if you have one.

Honey Whole-Wheat Bread

If you don't have the time to make the real thing, try this variation of our Honey Whole-Wheat Bread. It's not bad, all in all!

YIELD: ONE 1½-POUND LOAF

1¼ cups milk
1 tablespoon extra-virgin olive oil
2½ cups whole-wheat flour
½ cup unbleached all-purpose flour
⅓ cup honey
1 teaspoon salt
2 teaspoons active dry yeast

Carefully measure all the ingredients into the bread-machine pan, and follow the manufacturer's instructions. If your machine has a whole-wheat setting, use it. Set for a light crust and an extended rise.

Seven-Grain Whole-Wheat Bread

This loaf has seven-grain cereal mix added for extra crunch. (If you can find nine-grain, that's all right, too.) The grains included are usually four to six varieties of wheat, as well as a mix of triticale, rye, barley, oats, and/or millet. The cereal needs to be soaked at least 8 hours, or overnight, before you can make this bread. I've made an exception to my "oil instead of butter" rule for this loaf.

YIELD: ONE 1½-POUND LOAF

½ cup seven-grain cereal mix

1½ cups skim milk

2 tablespoons unsalted butter

2 cups unbleached all-purpose flour

1 cup whole-grain flour

3 tablespoons honey

1½ teaspoons salt

2 teaspoons active dry yeast

Soak the seven-grain cereal mix in water to cover overnight. Drain well.

Carefully measure all the ingredients into the bread-machine pan, and follow the manufacturer's instructions. If your machine has a whole-wheat setting, use it. Set for a light crust and an extended rise.

Cinnamon, Raisin, and Walnut Whole-Wheat Bread

We make CRW (as we call it at the stores) on a daily basis. It's a dense bread that adapts well to the bread-machine process.

YIELD: A 1½-POUND LOAF

1 cup milk
2 large egg whites
¼ cup canola oil
1½ cups whole-wheat flour
1½ cups unbleached all-purpose flour
1 teaspoon ground cinnamon
¼ cup molasses
2 teaspoons active dry yeast
½ cup dark raisins
¼ cup coarsely chopped walnuts

Carefully measure all the ingredients into the bread-machine pan, and follow the manufacturer's instructions. If your machine has a "fruits and nuts" setting, add the raisins and walnuts at that time. If your machine has a whole-wheat setting, use it. Set for a light crust and an extended rise.

Garlic Cheese Bread

This is so nice to come home to when you have just enough time to throw together some pasta and sauce! This is a "tear apart" bread, not a slicing bread.

YIELD: A 1½-POUND LOAF

1¼ cups lukewarm water (90–95°F)

1 tablespoon extra-virgin olive oil

3½ cups unbleached all-purpose flour

1 tablespoon dried parsley flakes

1 teaspoon dried oregano leaves (not ground)

2 tablespoons grated Parmesan cheese

1 tablespoon chopped garlic in olive oil

1 tablespoon sugar

1 teaspoon salt

2 teaspoons active dry yeast

Carefully measure all the ingredients into the bread-machine pan, and follow the manufacturer's instructions. Set for a dark crust and use the extended-rise cycle.

Whole-Wheat Pizza

I think the bread machine is best used to prepare doughs for recipes other than loaf breads, like this whole-wheat pizza dough. Top it any way you want for a quick, satisfying meal.

YIELD: I LARGE PIZZA

I cup warm water (95–105°F)
2 tablespoons extra-virgin olive oil
2 cups whole-wheat flour
I cup unbleached all-purpose flour
I teaspoon honey
I teaspoon salt
I½ teaspoons active dry yeast
Topping of choice

Carefully measure all the ingredients into the bread-machine pan, and follow the manufacturer's instructions, choosing the "dough" setting. When the beeper sounds, remove the dough from the machine.

Preheat the oven to 450°F. Let the dough rest for 5 to 10 minutes. Prepare the topping of your choice. Shape the dough into a round to fit a large pizza pan or an 11×9-inch cookie sheet. Top the dough and bake for 15 to 18 minutes.

$\mathcal{M}$uffins and $\mathcal{Q}$uick $\mathcal{B}$reads

Our youngest child was four when I went to work full time and my husband took on the primary responsibility for child-rearing. We both went through profound changes, but it was the way our children viewed us that surprised us most of all.

Suddenly, Daddy was the one they called when they were hurt. They asked Dad where to put things. Most painful for me, Dad was the one who was there when they woke up and got them ready for school.

It wasn't always a smooth transition. I once came home from a long, long workday to find Scott at the door with his gym bag. "Where do you think you're going?" I demanded. He screamed back, "I need out! I don't have a life of my own any more!" In an instant we were both howling with laughter at how far we had come.

I tell this story to open this chapter because these quick treats are the kinds of breads that even Scott could handle: not too many ingredients, no need to have a "feel" for the dough, and a short time in the oven. It's almost-instant gratification for little people (and their folks).

Cherry-Almond Muffins

You can satisfy your sweet tooth by using maraschino cherries, or make these tart with sour or Bing cherries. Both are delicious in their own way. I once had a woman give me a twenty-minute lecture on how I would poison Massachusetts with the dye in the maraschino cherries. I hope she's found something more important to worry about!

Yield: 12 muffins

2 cups whole-wheat flour

½ cup sugar

2 teaspoons baking powder

1 teaspoon baking soda

2 large egg whites (¼ cup)

1 cup plain nonfat yogurt

2 teaspoons almond extract

1 cup halved maraschino cherries, well drained and halved, or canned
   sour or Bing cherries, well drained and halved

½ cup sliced almonds

Preheat the oven to 350°F. Spray thoroughly a 12-cup muffin tin.

In a large bowl, mix the flour, sugar, baking powder, and baking soda. In a medium-size bowl, beat the egg whites, then add the yogurt and almond extract and mix well. Add the egg white mixture to the flour mixture and mix until just combined. Fold in the cherries and almonds.

Fill the muffins cups two-thirds full. Bake for 16 to 18 minutes, or until a toothpick inserted in the center of a muffin comes out clean.

Turn out the muffins from the tin, and serve warm.

Blueberry-Peach Muffins

These are dense muffins, with the surprise of blueberries and peaches for a contrast in texture. Dice, don't mash, the peaches for the best results.

YIELD: 12 MUFFINS

1½ cups whole-wheat flour
½ cup unbleached all-purpose flour
⅓ cup sugar
2½ teaspoons baking powder
½ teaspoon baking soda
½ teaspoon ground cinnamon
2 large egg whites (¼ cup)
1 cup vanilla nonfat yogurt
½ cup fresh or thawed, drained frozen blueberries
½ cup diced fresh or well-drained canned peaches

Preheat the oven to 350°F. Spray thoroughly a 12-cup muffin tin.

In a large bowl, mix the flours, sugar, baking powder, baking soda, and cinnamon. In a medium-size bowl, beat the egg whites, then add the yogurt and mix well. Add the egg white mixture to the flour mixture and stir until just combined. Fold in the blueberries and peaches.

Fill the muffin cups two-thirds full. Bake for 16 to 18 minutes, or until a toothpick inserted in the center of a muffin comes out clean.

Turn out the muffins from the tin, and serve warm.

Lemon-Poppy Seed Muffins

This is a light muffin (as low-fat muffins go!) that will be lighter for each additional second you take to whip up the egg whites. You can substitute 1 teaspoon of lemon, vanilla, or almond extract for the lemon juice and zest if you prefer.

YIELD: 12 MUFFINS

1½ cups unbleached all-purpose flour
⅓ cup sugar
1½ teaspoons baking powder
1½ tablespoons poppy seeds
2 large egg whites (¼ cup)
¾ cup plain nonfat yogurt
1 tablespoon lemon juice
1 teaspoon grated lemon zest

Preheat the oven to 350°F. Spray thoroughly a 12-cup muffin tin.

In a large bowl, mix the flour, sugar, baking powder, and poppy seeds. In a medium-size bowl, beat the egg whites, then add the yogurt, lemon juice, and lemon zest. Add the egg white mixture to the flour mixture and stir until just combined.

Fill the muffin cups two-thirds full and bake for 14 to 17 minutes, or until a toothpick inserted in the center of a muffin comes out clean. Turn out the muffins from the tin, and serve warm.

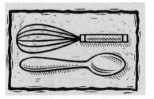

Apple-Raisin Muffins

A pleasant, filling muffin that travels well—perfect for lunchboxes and snack bags.

YIELD: 12 MUFFINS

2¼ cups whole-wheat flour
⅓ cup (packed) brown sugar
1½ teaspoons baking powder
4 large egg whites (½ cup)
¾ cup plain nonfat yogurt
I teaspoon vanilla extract
1½ cups peeled, chopped apples
½ cup dark raisins

Preheat the oven to 350°F. Spray thoroughly a 12-cup muffin tin.

In a large bowl, mix the flour, sugar, and baking powder. In a medium-size bowl, beat the egg whites, then add the yogurt, vanilla and apples. Add to the dry ingredients and stir with a spoon until just combined. Fold in the raisins.

Fill the muffin pans two-thirds full of batter. Bake for 16 to 18 minutes or until a toothpick inserted in the center of a muffin comes out clean. Turn the muffins out on a wire rack and allow to cool for 5 to 10 minutes. Serve warm or at room temperature.

Carrot Cake Muffins

This recipe, which was given to me years ago, contains almost no fat. To eliminate even more (but also a great deal of texture, and some flavor), you can leave out the almonds.

YIELD: 18 MUFFINS

1½ cups whole-wheat flour
½ cup unbleached all-purpose flour
¼ cup nonfat dry milk
1 teaspoon baking powder
½ teaspoon baking soda
½ tablespoon ground cinnamon
½ scant teaspoon freshly grated nutmeg
¼ teaspoon ground allspice
1 large egg white (⅛ cup)
½ cup mashed ripe banana
8 ounces frozen unsweetened apple juice concentrate, thawed
1 (8-ounce) can juice-packed crushed pineapple, drained
2½ cups grated carrots
¼ cup buttermilk
½ tablespoon vanilla extract
¼ cup chopped almonds
½ cup dark raisins

Preheat the oven to 400°F. Spray thoroughly three 6-cup muffin tins.

In a large bowl, combine the flours, nonfat dry milk, baking powder, baking soda, and spices. In a medium-size bowl, beat the egg white, then add the bananas, apple juice concentrate, pineapple, carrots, buttermilk, and vanilla and mix well. Add the banana mixture to the flour mixture and stir with a spoon until just combined. Fold in the almonds and raisins.

Fill the muffin pans three-fourths full. Bake 25 to 30 minutes or until a toothpick inserted in one of the muffins comes out clean. Cool the muffins in the tins for 8 to 10 minutes before removing them to wire racks to cool completely.

Fat-Free Fruit Spice Muffins

This is the first fat-free muffin that we produced at our stores. It's sugar-free, dairy-free, and the trace of fat in the recipe comes from the flour. It's very dense, fruitcake-like in texture (Don't let that put you off!), and a great, fruity, naturally sweet treat.

YIELD: 18 MUFFINS

2½ cups dark raisins

1 cup chopped dried apples

½ cup chopped dried apricots

½ cup dried cranberries

¼ cup chopped pitted dates

2½ cups hot water

5 cups whole-wheat flour

2 tablespoons baking powder

¼ cup ground cinnamon

1 cup egg substitute (such as Egg Beaters)

2 cups unsweetened applesauce

Preheat the oven to 350°F. Spray thoroughly three 6-cup muffin tins.

In a medium-size bowl, combine the raisins, apples, apricots, cranberries, and dates. Cover with the hot water, and soak for 10 to 15 minutes. Drain well.

In a large bowl, mix the flour, baking powder, and cinnamon. Add the drained fruit and toss until thoroughly coated. Add the egg substitute and applesauce and stir until just combined.

Fill the muffins cups to the top. Bake for 35 to 40 minutes, or until a toothpick inserted in the center of a muffin comes out clean. Allow to cool completely before turning out of the tins and serving.

Banana-Pineapple Muffins

This recipe must be made with very, very ripe bananas; the skins should be almost entirely black. Otherwise, the muffins will be quite flat and without flavor.

YIELD: 18 MUFFINS

4½ cups whole-wheat flour
2 tablespoons baking powder
¼ cup ground cinnamon
1 cup egg substitute (such as Egg Beaters)
¾ cup unsweetened applesauce
1 (20-ounce) can juice-packed crushed pineapple, drained
3 large, very ripe bananas, mashed

Preheat the oven to 350°F. Spray thoroughly three 6-cup muffin tins.

In a large bowl, mix the flour, baking powder, and cinnamon. In a medium-size bowl, stir the egg substitute, applesauce, pineapple, and bananas to mix well. Add the banana mixture to the flour mixture and stir until just combined.

Fill the muffins cups to the top. Bake for 35 to 40 minutes, or until a toothpick inserted in the center of a muffin comes out clean. Allow to cool completely in the tins before turning out of the tins and serving.

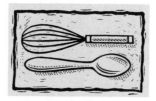

Irish Soda Bread

Where I live now, Irish soda bread is a very big deal. This is a traditional soda bread and a great recipe. Using light and dark raisins adds a nice color contrast, and I wouldn't dream of making Irish soda bread without caraway seeds.

YIELD: 1 LOAF

2 cups unbleached all-purpose flour

2 teaspoons baking soda

2 teaspoons baking powder

1 teaspoon salt

3 tablespoons sugar

3 tablespoons cold butter, cut into very small cubes

1 cup buttermilk

¼ cup dark raisins

¼ cup golden raisins

1½ tablespoons caraway seeds

1 large egg white

1 tablespoon water

Preheat the oven to 350°F.

In a large bowl, mix the flour, baking soda, baking powder, salt, and sugar. Using a pastry cutter or two knives, cut in the butter until pea-sized chunks form. Add the buttermilk, raisins, and caraway seeds and mix until just combined.

Turn the dough out onto a piece of waxed paper and knead for about a minute. Form into a round, fairly flat loaf and place on an ungreased cookie sheet. Cut a cross in the top.

In a small bowl, lightly beat the egg white and water and use to brush the top of the loaf. Bake for 35 to 40 minutes, or until a golden brown. Remove the loaf from the sheet to a wire rack to cool completely.

Cranberry-Orange Quick Bread

This loaf can be made with any kind of white flour, but I prefer the texture and lightness that comes from using cake or pastry flour. I suspect you will, too. If you can't find orange oil, you can substitute an equal amount of orange extract, or 2 teaspoons of grated orange zest.

YIELD: ONE 9×5-INCH LOAF

2 cups white flour, preferably cake flour (not self-rising) or pastry flour
2½ teaspoons baking powder
2½ teaspoons baking soda
½ teaspoon salt
I cup coarsely chopped fresh or frozen cranberries
¼ teaspoon orange oil
I¼ cups orange juice
½ cup honey
¼ cup canola oil

Preheat the oven to 375°F. Spray a 9×5×3-inch loaf pan.

In a large bowl, mix the flour, baking powder, baking soda, and salt. In a medium-size bowl, stir the cranberries, orange oil, orange juice, honey, and oil to mix well. Add the cranberry mixture to the flour mixture and stir until just combined.

Spread the batter evenly in the prepared loaf pan and bake for 55 to 65 minutes, or until a toothpick inserted in the center comes out clean.

Cool the loaf in the pan on a wire rack for 10 minutes, then turn out of the pan onto the rack to cool completely.

Apple Quick Bread

This bread is quick to make and quick to disappear. It is crumbly, so I can't recommend it for your kid's lunchbox, but it tastes yummy!

YIELD: ONE 9×5-INCH LOAF

3 cups whole-wheat flour
¾ cup (packed) dark brown sugar
1½ teaspoons baking soda
1⅓ cups unsweetened apple juice
1½ teaspoons vanilla extract
3 cups chopped apples (peeled or unpeeled, it's up to you)
⅓ cup coarsely chopped pecans

Preheat the oven to 325°F. Spray thoroughly a 9×5×3-inch loaf pan.

In a large bowl, mix the flour, sugar, and baking soda. In a medium-size bowl, combine the apple juice, vanilla, apples, and pecans. Add the apple mixture to the flour mixture and stir until just combined.

Spread the batter evenly in the prepared loaf pan and bake for 55 to 65 minutes, or until a toothpick inserted in the center comes out clean. Cool the loaf in the pan on a wire rack for 10 minutes, then remove from the pan to the rack to cool completely.

Pumpkin Bread

Pumpkin has a bit of fat—more than most squashes, but still just a tad. It adds a lot of flavor but needs help from the pumpkin pie spice to keep it tasting like a treat. There is a bit of canola oil in this recipe to give it some added richness.

YIELD: ONE 9×5-INCH LOAF

2 cups cake flour (not self-rising) or white pastry flour
¾ cup sugar
I teaspoon baking soda
I teaspoon baking powder
I teaspoon salt
I½ teaspoons pumpkin pie spice
2 large egg whites (½ cup)
⅓ cup canola oil
⅓ cup molasses
I cup canned pumpkin (not pumpkin pie filling)
½ cup dark raisins (optional)
½ cup coarsely chopped walnuts (optional)

Preheat the oven to 350°F. Spray thoroughly a 9×5×3-inch loaf pan.

In a large bowl, mix the flour, sugar, baking soda, baking powder, salt, and pumpkin pie spice. In a medium-size bowl, beat the egg whites, then add the oil, molasses, and pumpkin and beat well. Add the pumpkin mixture to the flour mixture and stir with a spoon until just combined. Fold in the raisins and walnuts, if using.

Pour the batter into the prepared loaf pan and bake for I hour 10 minutes, or until a toothpick inserted in the center comes out clean. Cool the loaf in the pan on a wire rack for 10 minutes, then turn out onto the rack to cool completely.

Orphans

*S*ome of these recipes we enjoy at home, some we offer at Boston Daily Bread. I couldn't figure out where else they should go in the book, so here they are!

Cabbage Pockets

I grew up in Sterling, Colorado, an old railroad town settled by German and Polish immigrants. My friend Jeannie Kalinowski, whose family was German and Polish, ate the best food in town. Her mother made fruit dumplings and sweet pastries and homemade noodles. Jeannie called these "beerocks"; when my mom made them we called them "cabbage pockets." My husband and father like to take these on camping trips because they're just as good cold as they are hot.

At our house, we spread butter over the hot pockets. You may be more restrained.

YIELD: 5 LARGE POCKETS

Two recipes Peasant White Bread dough (page 32)
1 pound very lean ground beef or turkey
4 cups coarsely chopped cabbage
2 cups coarsely chopped onion
1 tablespoon salt
1 tablespoon pepper

While the dough is rising for the first time, brown the meat, cabbage, and onion in a nonstick skillet. Drain well and cool to room temperature. Season to taste with salt and pepper.

When the dough is risen, divide it into 5 sections (about 8 ounces each). On a well-floured board, roll or flatten each piece of dough into a 10 × 10-inch square. Place ½ cup of the filling mixture on one half of one dough square. Fold the other dough half over the filling and seal the pocket by pinching the edges hard. Repeat with the remaining dough squares and filling.

Place the pocket on a greased cookie sheet and let rise, covered, in a warm place for 20 minutes.

Preheat the oven to 350°F.

Bake the pockets for 18 to 20 minutes, until browned.

Fat-Free Sticky Buns

To make these sticky buns (where I come from we call them cinnamon rolls, but I defer to the customs of my adopted state, Massachusetts), we substitute honey for butter. But what the heck, take a chance once in a while, and use a pastry brush to thinly spread some melted butter over the dough.

YIELD: 16 BUNS

1 recipe Peasant White Bread (page 32) or Honey Whole-Wheat Bread
   (page 56)
1 cup honey
2 tablespoons ground cinnamon
2 cups dark raisins
½ cup coarsely chopped walnuts
1 cup confectioners' sugar
2 teaspoons orange juice

While the dough is rising, in a medium-size bowl mix the honey, cinnamon, raisins, and walnuts.

Spray thoroughly a 13×9×2-inch baking pan.

Divide the dough in 2 equal pieces. Roll out half the dough to a rectangle 14 to 16 inches long and 8 to 10 inches wide. Spread half the honey mixture evenly over the dough. Beginning with the short edge closest to you, roll the dough up tightly. Pinch the seam closed and slice the roll into 1-inch pieces. Place the pieces, cut side up, in the baking pan, edges touching.

Repeat with the second piece of dough and remaining filling.

Let the buns rise, covered, in a warm place for 25 minutes.

Preheat the oven to 350°F.

Bake the buns for 16 to 18 minutes, until the edges are lightly browned. Remove rolls from the oven and let them cool in the pan on a wire rack.

In a small bowl, mix the confectioners' sugar and orange juice until smooth. When the buns are cool, frost lightly with the sugar and orange juice mixture.

Grandma-to-Be's Bread Pudding

My memories of bread pudding go back to Delavan, Wisconsin, where my paternal grandmother made this special dessert for us whenever we would visit from Colorado.

Every Saturday Grandma Flahive would clean out the refrigerator, and into the skillet went anything that would go through the hand grinder bolted to the counter—pot roast, potatoes, onions, carrots. . . . But after her skillet hash came her wonderful, cinnamon-scented bread pudding, hot from the oven.

Try this low-fat version of Grandma's dessert, hot or cold, and create some family memories of your own

YIELD: 9 SERVINGS

6 cups cubed leftover bread (white, wheat, seven-grain, cinnamon-walnut-raisin, anything as long as it doesn't have garlic or onion in it!)
½ cup dark raisins
5 large egg whites (⅝ cup)
1 cup mashed ripe banana
⅓ cup honey
1½ cups skim milk
½ teaspoon ground cinnamon, plus additional for sprinkling
⅛ teaspoon grated nutmeg
⅛ teaspoon ground allspice
1 teaspoon vanilla extract

Spray thoroughly an 8×8-inch baking pan.

In a large bowl, mix the bread and raisins. In a medium-size bowl, beat the egg whites, then add the bananas, honey, milk, ½ teaspoon cinnamon, the nutmeg, allspice, and vanilla. Pour over the bread and raisin mixture, and let soak for 15 minutes.

Preheat the oven to 350°F.

Pour the pudding mixture into the baking pan, sprinkle lightly with cinnamon, and bake for 55 to 60 minutes, or until a knife or toothpick inserted in the center comes out clean.

Let the pudding cool for 5 to 10 minutes. Serve warm. Leftovers can be refrigerated.

Chocolate Cake

This wonderful, moist, and very rich cake is simple to make and contains no dairy products. It has a dense, brownie-like texture.

YIELD: ONE 11 × 9-INCH CAKE

4 cups unbleached all-purpose flour
4 cups sugar
½ cup unsweetened cocoa powder
1 tablespoon baking soda
1 teaspoon salt
⅓ cup canola oil
2 cups water
3 tablespoons vanilla extract
2 tablespoons vinegar

Preheat the oven to 350°F. Spray thoroughly an 11×9×2-inch cake pan.

In a large bowl, mix the flour, sugar, cocoa powder, baking soda, and salt. In a medium-size bowl beat the oil, the water, vanilla, and vinegar. Make a well in the flour mixture, add the oil mixture, and stir for about 2 minutes. There may still be some small lumps, but they'll disappear during baking.

Pour the batter into the prepared cake pan and bake for 30 to 35 minutes, or until a toothpick inserted in the center comes out clean.

Cool the cake in the pan on a wire rack before slicing.

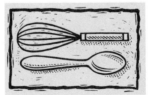

Raisin Bran Cookies

YIELD: 24 COOKIES

1 cup wheat bran

1¼ cups water

1 cup plus 2 tablespoons whole-wheat flour

2 teaspoons baking powder

¼ teaspoon baking soda

1½ teaspoons salt

1½ teaspoons ground cinnamon

¾ teaspoon ground allspice

1 stick (½ cup) soya margarine

3 tablespoons molasses

½ cup honey

2 large egg whites (¼ cup), lightly beaten

6 tablespoons plain nonfat yogurt

1 cup dark raisins

Preheat the oven to 350°F. Spray cookie sheets thoroughly.

In a small bowl, combine the wheat bran and the water and let soak for 30 minutes.

In a medium-size bowl, mix the flour, baking powder, baking soda, salt, cinnamon, and allspice. In a large bowl, beat the margarine, molasses, and honey. Add the bran mixture, egg whites, and yogurt and stir well. Add the flour mixture and stir until well combined. Fold in the raisins.

Drop the dough by tablespoonfuls onto the prepared cookie sheets and bake for 13 to 15 minutes. Let cool on the sheets for about 2 minutes, then transfer to wire racks to cool completely.

Pineapple Upside-Down Cake

This is a lightened-up version of traditional Pineapple Upside-Down Cake. The fruits and juice make the self-contained icing. The cake is best served just 10 or 15 minutes out of the oven.

YIELD: 9 SERVINGS

1 (15-ounce) can juice-packed pineapple slices, well drained
1 maraschino cherry per pineapple slice, stemmed and drained
¼ cup frozen orange juice concentrate, thawed
½ cup (packed) brown sugar
1½ cups cake flour (not self-rising) or white pastry flour
1½ teaspoons baking powder
½ cup granulated sugar
1 large egg white
½ cup skim milk
½ cup honey
1½ teaspoons vanilla extract

Preheat the oven to 350°F. Spray thoroughly an 8×8×2-inch cake pan.

Arrange the pineapple slices over the bottom of the cake pan. Place a maraschino cherry in the center of each pineapple slice. Pour the orange juice over the fruit, and sprinkle the brown sugar over all.

In a large bowl, mix the flour, baking powder, and sugar. In a medium-size bowl, beat the egg white. Add the milk, honey, and vanilla and beat well. Add the egg white mixture to the flour mixture and stir for 2 to 2½ minutes, or until the ingredients are smooth and well combined. Spread the batter evenly over the fruit. Tap the pan on the counter a couple of times to remove any air bubbles.

Bake for 30 to 35 minutes, or until a toothpick inserted in the center comes out clean. Cool the cake in the pan on a wire rack for 5 to 10 minutes, then invert onto a serving plate. Let cool completely before serving.

Losing Our Way

This chapter is full of goodies that are full of fat. The cookies and scones we sell in our shops are not nonfat, and we let people know it with big signs.

Our culture does strange things to us about food. As more and more companies have come out with more reduced-fat and nonfat foods, people have allowed themselves to eat entire boxes of doughnuts or cookies just because they were labeled low-fat!

My mother-in-law had four grandsons first. She followed them around, shoving food into their mouths. If they left a bite of a sandwich, she would stalk them until they weren't paying attention and then slip it in, followed by a chaser of milk or juice. She'd repeat this process until every crumb was gone. After all, you bragged about how big your grandsons were and how much the mother's back hurt to carry around such a big boy.

But when her first granddaughter came along the rules changed. Kylie Mara was born with a metabolism that raced about fifty percent higher than anyone else's, and she ate that much more to compensate. At first, Nana just said, "What a good eater." Then it changed to, "You should be watching what she eats," and finally, with all seriousness, "Cindi, I think you need to get her to a doctor. I hear there are still tapeworms, you know!"

Our society has put an emphasis on women's thinness that becomes increasingly destructive. We eat to both reward and punish ourselves as men and women. The bottom line is: Don't let food make you crazy.

While it is satisfying and pleasing and can be loving, it is, first and last, sustaining. It is fuel, so try not to eat to make yourself happy—or deny yourself to help you feel superior.

These recipes are treats, things to savor because of their richness but not to eat all the time. They have a touch of luxury and indulgence and help to find the "balance" in a balanced diet.

Joanne's Date Bread

I think dates are most unappreciated. We use them in several items in our stores, but this is a recipe like the one we used at my house at Christmas when I was growing up.

YIELD: TWO 9×5-INCH LOAVES

3 cups unbleached all-purpose flour
1 tablespoon baking soda
½ teaspoon salt
2 cups coarsely chopped walnuts
½ cup shortening
1½ cups hot water
2 cups coarsely chopped, pitted dates
4 large eggs
2 teaspoons vanilla extract
2 cups sugar

Preheat the oven to 350°F. Spray thoroughly two 9×5×3-inch loaf pans.

In a large bowl, mix the flour, baking soda, salt, and walnuts. In a large bowl, beat the shortening, water, and dates for about 2 minutes. Add the eggs, vanilla, and sugar and beat well. Add the date mixture to the flour mixture and stir with a spoon until just combined.

Divide the batter evenly between the 2 prepared loaf pans and bake for 1 hour, or until a toothpick inserted in the center of a loaf comes out clean. Cool for 10 minutes in the pans on a wire rack, then turn the loaves out onto the rack to cool completely.

Cherry-Coconut Quick Loaf

This bread isn't low fat, but the fat doesn't come from the toasted coconut. The coconut adds flavor, but if you're feeling guilty, save this special bread for an occasion.

YIELD: ONE 9×5-INCH LOAF

I cup shredded coconut
2 cups unbleached all-purpose flour
¾ cup sugar
2 teaspoons baking powder
½ teaspoon salt
I large egg
I cup milk
¼ cup (½ stick) butter, melted
I teaspoon almond extract
I cup halved maraschino cherries, 3 halves reserved for garnish

Preheat the oven to 450°F. Spray thoroughly a 9×5×3-inch loaf pan.

Spread the coconut on a cookie sheet and toast in the oven for 8 to 10 minutes, or until lightly browned. Let the coconut cool. Reduce the oven heat to 350°F.

In a large bowl, mix the toasted coconut, flour, sugar, baking powder, and salt. In a medium-size bowl, beat the egg, then add the milk, butter, and almond extract and beat well. Add the egg mixture to the flour mixture, and stir until just combined. Fold in the maraschino cherries.

Spread the batter in the prepared pan. Garnish with the reserved cherry halves. Bake for I hour, or until a toothpick inserted in the center comes out clean.

Cool the loaf in the pan on a wire rack for 10 minutes, then remove from the pan to the rack to cool completely.

Baking Powder Biscuits

You can use these as a base for strawberry or raspberry shortcake, or you can enjoy them hot from the oven with plenty of sweet butter. I like to sprinkle these biscuits with large-grained granulated sugar so they sparkle like sugar cookies.

YIELD: 8 TO 10 BISCUITS

2 cups unbleached all-purpose flour
I tablespoon sugar
I tablespoon baking powder
½ teaspoon salt
5 tablespoons (⅔ stick) cold lightly salted butter, cut into small cubes
⅔ cup milk

Preheat the oven to 400°F.

In a large bowl, mix the flour, sugar, baking powder, and salt. With a pastry cutter or two knives, cut the butter into the flour mixture until small pea-sized chunks form. Add the milk and stir until a soft dough forms.

Turn the dough onto a lightly floured work surface and knead 12 to 15 times. Roll the dough out to a thickness of ½ inch and cut into biscuits with a plain 3-inch biscuit cutter.

Place the biscuits on an ungreased cookie sheet. Brush the tops with a little milk and sprinkle with some granulated sugar, if desired. Bake for 12 to 14 minutes, or until golden brown. Serve hot.

Cranberry-Orange Scones

When we first opened the store, I went to a local yoga center twice a week to get myself centered. One of the masters, a gorgeous guy with a heart of gold and a wonderful physique, came in for a scone and a cup of coffee every morning. After about six months, he came in and read the sign next to the scones that said "Not low fat" and said, "I've been wondering where I picked up these extra ten pounds!" So make these for an occasional treat or serve them at a special tea—not every day!

YIELD: 8 SCONES

⅔ cup heavy cream
½ cup sugar
1 large egg
1 teaspoon orange extract
3 cups sifted unbleached all-purpose flour
4 teaspoons baking powder
½ teaspoon salt
½ cup (1 stick) lightly salted cold butter, cut into small cubes
1 cup fresh or frozen cranberries
1 large egg white
1 tablespoon water

Preheat the oven to 350°F.

In a small bowl, beat together the cream, egg, and orange extract and set aside.

In a large bowl, combine the flour, sugar, baking powder, and salt. Add the butter and with a pastry cutter or two knives and cut in the butter until the mixture is the size of small peas. Add the cream mixture and mix until the ingredients are just combined. Fold in the cranberries.

In a small bowl, beat the egg white and water.

Drop the dough by heaping tablespoonfuls onto an ungreased baking sheet. Or roll out the dough ½ inch thick. Cut into eight equal pie shaped pieces. Brush the scones with the egg wash.

Bake for 18 to 20 minutes, or until the scones are golden brown. Remove from the oven and let cool on the baking sheet.

Hot Cross Scones

At Boston Daily Bread we make hot cross buns with a yeast dough, but I make these at home for a quick Easter treat. It's just a biscuit . . . with a twist!

YIELD: ABOUT 8 SCONES

SCONES:

2¼ cups unbleached all-purpose flour

¼ cup granulated sugar

I tablespoon baking powder

½ teaspoon salt

I teaspoon ground cinnamon

¼ teaspoon ground cloves

¼ teaspoon ground allspice

½ cup (I stick) cold lightly salted butter, cut into small cubes

½ cup golden raisins

¼ cup chopped dried apricots

⅔ cup milk

ICING:

¼ cup confectioners' sugar

I teaspoon orange juice

Preheat the oven to 375°F.

In a large bowl, mix the flour, granulated sugar, baking powder, salt, cinnamon, cloves, and allspice. With a pastry cutter or two knives, cut the butter into the flour mixture until small pea-sized chunks form. Add the fruit and milk and stir until a soft dough forms.

Turn the dough onto a lightly floured work surface and knead about 10 times. Roll the dough out to a thickness of ½ inch and cut out into scones with a plain 3-inch biscuit cutter.

Transfer the scones to an ungreased cookie sheet and bake for 12 to 15 minutes. Cool the scones on the cookie sheet.

In a small bowl, stir the confectioners' sugar and orange juice until smooth. Using a spoon, drip the icing onto each scone in the form of a cross.

Raspberry Streusel Muffins

I can't remember having a fresh raspberry until I lived in Montana. In late July, the famous Flathead Lake raspberries ripened and were available for four dollars a flat at the local IGA.

What luxury! I would buy four or five flats and spend a day canning jars of raspberry jam that would last us until the next summer.

Now I live in Massachusetts and pay four-fifty for half a pint of berries and hope that bottom layer hasn't started to mold.

If you have access to a bounty of fresh raspberries or blackberries, try this muffin!

YIELD: 12 MUFFINS

MUFFINS:

2 cups unbleached all-purpose flour
½ cup sugar
I tablespoon baking powder
¼ teaspoon baking soda
½ teaspoon salt
I large egg
¼ cup (½ stick) butter, melted
½ cup skim milk
½ cup fat-free sour cream
I teaspoon vanilla extract
I½ cups fresh raspberries

STREUSEL:

½ cup sugar
⅓ cup unbleached all-purpose flour
¼ cup butter, softened but not squishy

Preheat the oven to 400°F. Spray thoroughly a 12-cup muffin tin.

In a large bowl, mix the flour, sugar, baking powder, baking soda, and salt.

In a medium-size bowl, beat the egg, then add the melted butter, milk, sour cream, and vanilla and mix well. Add the egg mixture to the flour mixture and stir with a spoon until just combined and the dry ingredients are moistened. Fold in the raspberries.

In a small bowl, combine the sugar, flour, and butter for the streusel until crumbly.

Fill the muffin cups three-fourths full with the batter. Top with the streusel mixture. Bake for 18 to 20 minutes, or until a toothpick inserted in a muffin comes out clean. Carefully remove the muffins from the tin and serve warm.

Rhubarb Streusel Muffins

I love rhubarb! In Wisconsin, where my parents' people still live, they call it the pie plant. I've been promised a new cutting to plant at my new house in Massachusetts. Use the pink, narrow stalks for the best flavor and color (But don't touch the leaves—they're poisonous!). If you've got too much to use at once, keep it in your freezer to enjoy throughout the year.

YIELD: 12 MUFFINS

MUFFINS:

2 cups unbleached all-purpose flour
½ cup granulated sugar
1 heaping tablespoon baking powder
½ teaspoon salt
¼ teaspoon ground cinnamon
2 large eggs
1 cup milk
¼ cup (½ stick) butter, melted
2 cups diced rhubarb
1 teaspoon vanilla extract

STREUSEL:

½ cup (packed) brown sugar
⅓ cup unbleached all-purpose flour
¼ cup (½ stick) butter
¼ cup finely chopped walnuts

Preheat the oven to 375°F. Spray thoroughly a 12-cup muffin tin. In a large bowl, mix the flour, granulated sugar, baking powder, salt, and cinnamon. In a medium-size bowl, beat the eggs, then add the milk and butter and beat well. Stir in the rhubarb and vanilla. Add the rhubarb mixture to the flour mixture and stir until just combined.

In a small bowl, mix the brown sugar, flour, butter, and walnuts until crumbly.

Fill the prepared muffin cups three-fourths full with the batter. Top each muffin with a tablespoonful of streusel mixture. Bake for 15 to 18 minutes, or until a toothpick inserted in the center of a muffin comes out clean. Turn the muffins out of the tin to a wire rack to cool.

Black Forest Muffins

Whoever first put chocolate and cherry together knew how to top perfection!

YIELD: 12 MUFFINS

4 cups unbleached all-purpose flour
1½ cups sugar
1 package (12 ounces) chocolate chips
1½ tablespoons baking powder
¼ teaspoon baking soda
1 teaspoon salt
2 large eggs
¾ cup canola oil
1½ teaspoons vanilla extract
2 cups sour cream
3 cups fresh or drained canned Bing cherries, pitted

Preheat the oven to 375°F. Spray thoroughly a 12-cup muffin tin.

In a large bowl, combine the flour, sugar, chocolate chips, baking powder, baking soda, and salt. In a medium-size bowl beat the eggs, then add the oil, vanilla, and sour cream and beat well. Add the egg mixture to the flour mixture and stir until just combined. Fold in the cherries.

Fill the prepared muffin cups with the batter. Bake for 25 to 30 minutes, or until a toothpick inserted into the center of a muffin comes out clean (except for the melted chocolate). Turn the muffins out onto a wire rack to cool completely.

Raspberry-Ricotta Muffins

My very first employee, Theresa Kelliher, developed this muffin, which isn't that low in fat but is high in taste. It was a hit from the first time we offered it in the store. Theresa has gone on to play in a rock and roll band, but we think of her each time we make these muffins. You can substitute blackberry or peach jam for the raspberry jam. Don't eat these hot or you'll burn yourself on the jam!

YIELD: 12 MUFFINS

2 cups unbleached all-purpose flour
1 tablespoon baking powder
¼ teaspoon baking soda
½ cup sugar
1 large egg
⅓ cup (⅔ stick) butter, melted
½ cup skim milk
½ cup fat-free sour cream
½ cup raspberry jam
½ cup ricotta cheese

Preheat the oven to 400°F. Spray thoroughly a 12-cup muffin tin.

In a large bowl, mix the flour, baking powder, baking soda, and sugar. In a medium-size bowl, beat the egg, then add the melted butter, milk, and sour cream and beat well. Add the egg mixture to the flour mixture and stir with a spoon until just combined and the dry ingredients are moistened.

Fill the muffin cup a little less than half full, using about half the batter. With the back of a spoon, make a well in the batter, and place 2 scant teaspoons each of jam and ricotta in the well. Add the remaining batter, making sure the jam-ricotta filling is covered.

Bake for 18 to 20 minutes, until the tops of the muffins are browned. Cool the muffins, in the pan on a wire rack.

Oatmeal Cookies

This is a sweet, fruity cookie recipe that stays moist for days. Toasting the coconut for 6 to 8 minutes spread thin on an ungreased cookie sheet in a 375°F oven will add wonderful flavor to the cookies but is optional.

YIELD: 18 COOKIES

I cup unbleached all-purpose flour
¾ teaspoon baking soda
I teaspoon salt
I½ teaspoons ground cinnamon
½ teaspoon grated nutmeg
I cup (2 sticks) butter, softened
I½ cups (packed) brown sugar
½ cup granulated sugar
I large egg
I½ teaspoons vanilla extract
½ cup water
I½ cups rolled oats
¾ cup dark raisins
⅓ cup shredded coconut

Preheat the oven to 350°F. Spray thoroughly 2 cookie sheets.

In a medium-size bowl, stir the flour, baking soda, salt, cinnamon, and nutmeg. In a large bowl, beat the butter and sugars, then add the egg, vanilla, and water and beat well. Add the flour mixture and stir well to combine. Add the oats, raisins, and coconut and mix well.

Drop the dough by heaping tablespoonfuls onto the prepared cookie sheets and bake for 10 to 12 minutes, or until the cookies are lightly browned. Let cool on the sheets for 2 to 3 minutes, then remove the cookies to wire racks to cool completely.

Spreading the Wealth

BOSTON DAILY BREAD became more than a bread store shortly after we got our feet on the ground. Our wheat producer, Wheat Montana Farms, gave our name to people who had the same ideas about bread baking and were seeking out consulting services. After I felt we had changed our original recipes so they gave consistent results and, more important, tasted great, I signed our first consulting agreement and went out on the road.

From the first store in Madison, Wisconsin, to the most recent investigations into stores in Vietnam and Romania, our breads have become international in their appeal. I have helped lawyers and psychologists, airline pilots and athletic shoe salesmen open low-fat, whole-grain bread stores and change their lives. None of these folks had ever worked in the food business, and few of them had ever baked at home, but they all came with the passion for the product and the passion for the idea of spending their lives making and selling something wholesome and pure.

When each of these people is preparing to open their store, I have the privilege to travel to that part of the country. I always leave a day before our training begins to drive around, check out the antique stores, and try to discover something about the people who live in the area. I can remember stopping at the edge of a field in Minnesota as two children rode by on their bikes with a dog chasing behind, brilliant yellow and green corn in the field below them and red silos and blue sky rising behind them. It was a moment of grace and purity I will never forget.

I passed the real "Walton's Mountain" and Walton's General Store while working in the store in Charlottesville, Virginia. I visited the East Bay next to San Francisco after the wettest spring they had experienced in years and was staggered by lush roses and rolling, grass-covered hills that were as green as those in Ireland. I have come back from all twenty-five trips thrilled to have had the opportunity to visit and experience the wonders this country has to offer.

And as I travel and meet folks on airplanes, at rental car counters and in hotel lobbies, I will mention why I'm visiting. The conversation invariably brings an answering smile and an insistent "When's it opening? Where's the store? We've been waiting for something like this!"

At it's simplest, bread is the basis of our lives. Whether storebought or homebaked, coming together over a loaf of bread is to honor the union of body and spirit. We use bread as nourishment for our bodies. We also use it to celebrate and even represent the deity. In sharing bread with others, or abstaining from bread on a fast, we've let our God know that we need that deity to nourish our souls as bread nourishes our bodies. Each faith has rituals that center around the table, rituals that celebrate the importance of eating and drinking together in the presence and love of God.

When I first started this business, I saw it as a life raft. We were adrift, having been cut loose by corporate America. All of the subconscious messages that I've now had the time to reflect on weren't clear when my journey as a baker began. There have also been some messages from professionals who love to buy our bread and smell the smells in the store. But they say, "You *chose* to be a baker?" with a sneer in their voice. Have we come to a point where a profession where we get our hands messy is less valuable than wearing a suit and sitting behind a computer?

As I speak with people who are considering changing their lifestyle to one that involves physical work rather than desk work, I often wonder if I can convey to them how satisfying the hand making of bread can be. I come to their new store during the most stressful time in their lives, and we labor together to give birth to a new life for them in a new business. Like a parent, I walk away after giving them the skills and knowledge to live and work independently. When I leave, we exchange hugs with flour flying off hands and aprons, with the day's bread finishing in the oven, and then they move on to help the next customer as I leave through the back door unnoticed. But what I have left is powerful: I have passed on the knowledge of how to make love— with flour, water, yeast, and salt.

Here is a list of bakeries that I have assisted in spreading the good news of homestyle bread baking. The list is growing all the time, so write to me at Boston Daily Bread for an updated list.

Boston Daily Bread of Sudbury
505 Boston Post Road
Sudbury, MA 01776
508/443-7474

Boston Daily Bread
1331 Beacon Street
Brookline, MA 02146
617/277-8801

Bread Barn
High Point Center
7475 Mineral Point Road
Madison, WI 53717
608/833-5965

Bread Barn
Lake Zurich, IL
847/350-0083

Spring Mill Bread Company
4961 Elm Street
Bethesda, MD 20814
301/654-7970

Spring Mill II
12187 Darnestown Road
Gaithersburg, MD 20878
301/977-7733

The Bread Company
2700 West College Avenue
Appleton, WI 54914
414/739-4350

Stone Mill Bread Company
Thruway Shopping Center
272 South Stratford Road
Winston-Salem, NC 27103
910/721-0567

Carolina Country Bread
2168 Lawndale Shopping Center
Greensboro, NC 27408
910/854-5883

Bread Baker Company
Miracle Mile Center
16 17th Street NW
Rochester, MN 55904
507/289-7052

Bread Baker Company
Tower Square
582 Prairie Center Drive
Eden Prairie, MN 55344
612/996-9444

Harvest Home Bread Company by
    Grannie Annie
23369 Lyons Avenue
Valencia, CA 91355
805/254-8989

Breaking Bread
1428 South Milwaukee
Libertyville, IL 60048
708/816-4707

Healthy Harvest Bread Company
9110 Alcosta Boulevard
San Ramon, CA 94588
510/829-5236

Fields of Grain Bread Store
1905 Rio Hill Center
Charlottesville, VA 22901
804/432-0289

Prairie Bread Kitchen
103 North Marion
Oak Park, IL 60301

$\int$ources

OUR FINE GRAINS are grown by Wheat Montana Farms. They will be happy to provide you with the customer closest to where you are if you contact them at:

> Wheat Montana Farms
> P.O. Box 4778
> Helena, MT 59604
> or call 800/535-2798
> or fax 406/443-3910

For information on Breadwinner's Consulting, contact:

> Breadwinner's Consulting
> 19 Darvell Drive
> Sudbury, MA 01776
> or call 508/443-7474
> or fax 508/440-9666

Home grain mills:

Magic Mill
235 West 200 South
Salt Lake City, UT 84101

Notes

Notes

Notes

Notes

Index

all-purpose flour, 17–18
Almond-Cherry Muffins, 78
Anadama Bread, 42
apple:
    Cinnamon, and Raisin Loaf, 40
    Cinnamon Swirl Bread, 50
    Quick Bread, 88
    Raisin Muffins, 81

baking loaves, 25–26
baking powder, 19
    Biscuits, 103
baking soda, 19
banana:
    Grandma-to-Be's Bread Pudding, 94
    Pineapple Muffins, 85
beef, in Cabbage Pockets, 92
Biscuits, Baking Powder, 103
Blackberry-Ricotta Muffins, 113
Black Forest Muffins, 112
Blueberry-Peach Muffins, 79
Boston Daily Bread (Brookline, Mass.),
    115, 119
    origins of, 15–16, 30
Boston Daily Bread of Sudbury (Sud-
    bury, Mass.), 16, 119
boules, forming, 24
bowls, 21
bran:
    gluten film and, 28
    Raisin Cookies, 97

Bread Baker Co. (Eden Prairie, Minn.),
    120
Bread Baker Co. (Rochester, Minn.), 120
Bread Barn (Lake Zurich, Ill.), 119
Bread Barn (Madison, Wis.), 119
The Bread Company (Appleton, Wis.),
    120
bread flour, 17
bread-machine breads, 69–76
    author's disappointment with, 69
    Cinnamon, Raisin, and Walnut
        Whole-Wheat, 74
    Country White, 71
    Garlic Cheese, 75
    Honey Whole-Wheat, 72
    Seven-Grain Whole-Wheat, 73
    tips for, 70
    Whole-Wheat Pizza, 76
bread making, 23–28
    adding extra ingredients, 31
    baking loaves, 25–26
    checking for doneness, 25
    dividing dough, 24
    final rise (proofing), 25, 28
    first rise, 24
    forming loaves, 24
    fresh flour for, 30
    "good dough" in, 27–28, 31
    measuring, 23
    mixing dough, 23–24, 27–28
    rotating loaves during baking, 25, 26

bread pans, 2I–22
  getting dough into, 24
Bread Pudding, Grandma-to-Be's, 94
Breadwinner's Consulting, I23
breakfast fare:
  Apple-Cinnamon Swirl Bread, 50
  Apple Quick Bread, 88
  Challah, 48
  Cherry, Walnut, and Vanilla Whole-
    Wheat Bread, 64
  Cherry-Coconut Quick Loaf, I02
  Cinnamon, Apple, and Raisin Loaf,
    40
  Cinnamon, Raisin, and Walnut
    Whole-Wheat Bread (bread ma-
    chine), 74
  Cinnamon Swirl Bread, 44
  Cranberry-Orange Quick Bread,
    87
  Cranberry-Orange Scones, I04
  Fat-Free Sticky Buns, 93
  Hot Cross Scones, I06
  Irish Soda Bread, 86
  Joanne's Date Bread, I0I
  Pumpkin Bread, 89
  see also muffins
Breaking Bread (Libertyville, Ill.), I2I
browning, 25
Buns, Fat-Free Sticky, 93
butter, in bread-machine breads, 70

Cabbage Pockets, 92
cake(s):
  Carrot, Muffins, 82
  Chocolate, 96
  Pineapple Upside-Down, 98
Carolina Country Bread (Greensboro,
    N.C.), I20

carrot:
  Cake Muffins, 82
  Orange Whole-Wheat Bread, 62
  Tarragon Bread, 36
Challah, 48
Cheddar-Jalapeño Bread, 34
cheese:
  Cheddar-Jalapeño Bread, 34
  Garlic Bread (bread machine), 75
  Jack, Mushroom, and Parsley Whole-
    Wheat Bread, 58
  Ricotta-Raspberry Muffins, II3
  Swiss and Spinach Whole-Wheat
    Bread, 60
cherry(ies):
  Almond Muffins, 78
  Black Forest Muffins, II2
  Coconut Quick Loaf, I02
  Walnut, and Vanilla Whole-Wheat
    Bread, 64
chicken dishes, Carrot-Tarragon Bread as
    accompaniment for, 36
chocolate:
  Black Forest Muffins, II2
  Cake, 96
cinnamon:
  Apple, and Raisin Loaf, 40
  Fat-Free Sticky Buns, 93
  Grandma-to-Be's Bread Pudding, 94
  Raisin, and Walnut Whole-Wheat
    Bread (bread machine), 74
  Swirl Apple Bread, 50
  Swirl Bread, 44
Coconut-Cherry Quick Loaf, I02
coffee cans, as bread pans, 22
cookies:
  Oatmeal, II4
  Raisin Bran, 97

cookie sheets, 21
cornmeal, 18
    Anadama Bread, 42
Country White (bread machine), 71
cranberry:
    Orange Quick Bread, 87
    Orange Scones, 104

Date Bread, Joanne's, 101
Deal, David, 46
desserts:
    Chocolate Cake, 96
    Grandma-to-Be's Bread Pudding,
      94
    Oatmeal Cookies, 114
    Pineapple Upside-Down Cake, 98
    Raisin Bran Cookies, 97
dishtowels, 21
dividing dough, 24
doneness, checking for, 25
dough scrapers, plastic, 22

equipment, 21–22
    heavy-duty standing mixers, 21
    muffin tins, 22
    pans, 21–22

fat-free baked goods:
    Fruit Spice Muffins, 84
    Sticky Buns, 93
    see also low-fat baked goods
Fields of Grain Bread Store (Char-
    lottesville, Va.), 121
flour, 17–18
    all-purpose, 17–18
    bread, 17
    freshness of, 30
    rye, 18

flour (cont'd)
    source for, 123
    stone-ground whole-grain, 18
Focaccia, 46
forming loaves, 24
fruit:
    adding to dough, 31
    Spice Muffins, Fat-Free, 84
    see also specific fruits

Garlic Cheese Bread (bread machine), 75
glass bread pans, 21
gluten film, 27–28, 31
"good dough," 27–28, 31
Grandma-to-Be's Bread Pudding, 94

Harvest Home Bread Co. by Grannie
    Annie (Valencia, Calif.), 120–21
Healthy Harvest Bread Co. (San Ramon,
    Calif.), 121
herbs:
    adding to dough, 31
    Focaccia topped with, 46
"home," meaning of, 55
home grain mills, source for, 124
honey, 19
    in bread-machine breads, 70
    Oat Whole-Wheat Bread, 66
    Whole-Wheat Bread, 56
    Whole-Wheat Bread (bread machine),
      72
Hot Cross Scones, 106

ingredients, 17–20
    cornmeal, 18
    flour, 17–18, 30
    leavening, 18–19
    measuring, 23

ingredients (*cont'd*)

    rye, 18

    salt, 20

    sources for, 123–24

    sweeteners, 19

Irish Soda Bread, 86

Italian Focaccia, 46

Jack Cheese, Mushroom, and Parsley
    Whole-Wheat Bread, 58

Jalapeño-Cheddar Bread, 34

Joanne's Date Bread, 101

Kalinowski, Jeannie, 92

Kelliher, Theresa, 113

Kitchen-Aid, 21

kneading, 24

    before last rise in bread machines, 70

leavening, 18–19

Lemon–Poppy Seed Muffins, 80

loaf pans, 21

low-fat baked goods:

    Anadama Bread, 42

    Apple-Cinnamon Swirl Bread, 50

    Apple Quick Bread, 88

    Apple-Raisin Muffins, 81

    Banana-Pineapple Muffins, 85

    Blueberry-Peach Muffins, 79

    Cabbage Pockets, 92

    Carrot Cake Muffins, 82

    Carrot-Orange Whole-Wheat Bread,
        62

    Carrot-Tarragon Bread, 36

    Challah, 48

    Cherry, Walnut, and Vanilla Whole-
        Wheat Bread, 64

low-fat baked goods (*cont'd*)

    Cherry-Almond Muffins, 78

    Chocolate Cake, 96

    Cinnamon, Apple, and Raisin Loaf,
        40

    Cinnamon, Raisin, and Walnut
        Whole-Wheat Bread (bread ma-
        chine), 74

    Cinnamon Swirl Bread, 44

    Country White (bread machine), 71

    Cranberry-Orange Quick Bread, 87

    Fat-Free Fruit Spice Muffins, 84

    Fat-Free Sticky Buns, 93

    Focaccia, 46

    Garlic Cheese Bread (bread machine),
        75

    Grandma-to-Be's Bread Pudding, 94

    Honey-Oat Whole-Wheat Bread, 66

    Honey Whole-Wheat Bread, 56

    Honey Whole-Wheat Bread (bread
        machine), 72

    Irish Soda Bread, 86

    Jalapeño-Cheddar Bread, 34

    Lemon–Poppy Seed Muffins, 80

    Mushroom, Parsley, and Jack Cheese
        Whole-Wheat Bread, 58

    Outrageous Rye Bread, 52

    Peasant White Bread, 32

    Pineapple Upside-Down Cake, 98

    Pumpkin Bread, 89

    Raisin Bran Cookies, 97

    Seven-Grain Whole-Wheat Bread
        (bread machine), 73

    Sun-Dried Tomato and Olive Bread,
        38

    Swiss and Spinach Whole-Wheat
        Bread, 60

low-fat baked goods (*cont'd*)
  Whole-Wheat Pizza (bread machine),
    76

McClean, Dave, 46
Magic Mill, 124
margarine, in bread-machine breads, 70
measuring cups and spoons, 21, 22
measuring ingredients, 23
milk, dried, in bread-machine breads, 70
mixers, heavy-duty standing, 21
  mixing dough with, 24
mixing dough, 23–24
  "good dough" and, 27–28, 31
molasses, 19
  Anadama Bread, 42
muffins, 77–85
  Apple-Raisin, 81
  Banana-Pineapple, 85
  Black Forest, 112
  Blueberry-Peach, 79
  Carrot Cake, 82
  Cherry-Almond, 78
  Fat-Free Fruit Spice, 84
  Lemon–Poppy Seed, 80
  Raspberry-Ricotta, 113
  Raspberry Streusel, 108
  Rhubarb Streusel, 110
muffin tins, 22
Mushroom, Parsley, and Jack Cheese
  Whole-Wheat Bread, 58

no-fat cooking spray, 22

oat(meal):
  Cookies, 114
  Honey Whole-Wheat Bread, 66

oil, in bread-machine breads, 70
Olive and Sun-Dried Tomato Bread, 38
olive oil, in bread-machine breads, 70
onion, in Cabbage Pockets, 92
orange:
  Carrot Whole-Wheat Bread, 62
  Cranberry Quick Bread, 87
  Cranberry Scones, 104
O'Rourke, Mary Jo, 15
Outrageous Rye Bread, 52
"oven spring," 25
oven temperature, 25–26

pans, 21–22
  getting dough into, 24
Parmesan Cheese Garlic Bread (bread
    machine), 75
Parsley, Mushroom, and Jack Cheese
    Whole-Wheat Bread, 58
pastry brushes, 22
peach:
  Blueberry Muffins, 79
  Ricotta Muffins, 113
Peasant White Bread, 32
pineapple:
  Banana Muffins, 85
  Upside-Down Cake, 98
Pizza, Whole-Wheat (bread machine), 76
plastic dough scrapers, 22
pockets:
  Cabbage, 92
  Country White (bread machine), 71
Poppy Seed–Lemon Muffins, 80
potatoes, Focaccia topped with, 46
Prairie Bread Kitchen (Oak Park, Ill.),
    121
proofing, 25, 28

Pudding, Grandma-to-Be's Bread, 94
Pumpkin Bread, 89

quick breads, 77–89
  Apple, 88
  Baking Powder Biscuits, 103
  Cherry-Coconut Quick Loaf, 102
  Cranberry-Orange, 87
  Cranberry-Orange Scones, 104
  Hot Cross Scones, 106
  Irish Soda, 86
  Joanne's Date, 101
  Pumpkin, 89
  see also muffins

raisin(s):
  Apple Muffins, 81
  Bran Cookies, 97
  Cinnamon, and Apple Loaf, 40
  Cinnamon, and Walnut Whole-Wheat
    Bread (bread machine), 74
  Grandma-to-Be's Bread Pudding,
    94
raspberry:
  Ricotta Muffins, 113
  Streusel Muffins, 108
reduced-fat breads, see low-fat baked
  goods
Rhubarb Streusel Muffins, 110
Ricotta-Raspberry Muffins, 113
rising:
  final (proofing), 25, 28
  first, 24
rolling pins, 22
  forming loaves with, 24
rotating loaves during baking, 25,
  26
rubber spatulas, 22

rye, 18
  Bread, Outrageous, 52

salt, 20
sandwich breads:
  Carrot-Orange Whole-Wheat, 62
  Honey-Oat Whole-Wheat, 66
  Honey Whole-Wheat, 56
  Honey Whole-Wheat (bread ma-
    chine), 72
  Outrageous Rye, 52
  Peasant White, 32
  Seven-Grain Whole-Wheat (bread
    machine), 73
scones:
  Cranberry-Orange, 104
  Hot Cross, 106
Seven-Grain Whole-Wheat Bread (bread
  machine), 73
sheet pans, 21
Siniawski, Diane, 50
Soda Bread, Irish, 86
sources, 123–24
spatulas, rubber, 22
spice(s):
  adding to dough, 31
  Fruit Muffins, Fat-Free, 84
Spinach and Swiss Whole-Wheat Bread,
  60
spoons, wooden, 22
Spring Mill Bread Co. (Bethesda, Md.),
  119
Spring Mill II (Gaithersburg, Md.), 120
Sticky Buns, Fat-Free, 93
stone-ground whole-grain flour, 18
Stone Mill Bread Co. (Winston-Salem,
  N.C.), 120
straight doughs, 31

streusel muffins:
Raspberry, 108
Rhubarb, 110
sugar, 19
in bread-machine breads, 70
sun-dried tomato(es):
Focaccia topped with, 46
and Olive Bread, 38
sweeteners, 19
Swiss and Spinach Whole-Wheat Bread,
60

Tarragon-Carrot Bread, 36
teatime fare:
Apple Quick Bread, 88
Bran Raisin Cookies, 97
Cherry, Walnut, and Vanilla Whole-
Wheat Bread, 64
Cherry-Coconut Quick Loaf, 102
Cranberry-Orange Quick Bread, 87
Cranberry-Orange Scones, 104
Hot Cross Scones, 106
Irish Soda Bread, 86
Joanne's Date Bread, 101
Oatmeal Cookies, 114
Pumpkin Bread, 89
see also muffins
thermometers, 22
tomato(es), sun-dried:
Focaccia topped with, 46
and Olive Bread, 38
treats (higher-fat baked goods), 99–114
Baking Powder Biscuits, 103
Black Forest Muffins, 112
Cherry-Coconut Quick Loaf, 102
Cranberry-Orange Scones, 104
Hot Cross Scones, 106
Joanne's Date Bread, 101

treats (higher-fat baked goods) (cont'd)
Oatmeal Cookies, 114
Raspberry-Ricotta Muffins, 113
Raspberry Streusel Muffins, 108
Rhubarb Streusel Muffins, 110
turkey, in Cabbage Pockets, 92

Upside-Down Cake, Pineapple, 98

Vanilla, Cherry, and Walnut Whole-
Wheat Bread, 64
vegetables:
adding to dough, 31
see also specific vegetables

walnut(s):
Cherry, and Vanilla Whole-Wheat
Bread, 64
Cinnamon, and Raisin Whole-Wheat
Bread (bread machine), 74
Fat-Free Sticky Buns, 93
Wheat Montana Farms, 17, 115, 123
whisks, 22
white breads, 31–53
Anadama, 42
Apple-Cinnamon Swirl, 50
Carrot-Tarragon, 36
Challah, 48
Cinnamon, Apple, and Raisin Loaf,
40
Cinnamon Swirl, 44
Country (bread machine), 71
Focaccia, 46
Jalapeño-Cheddar, 34
making in bread machine, 70
Outrageous Rye, 52
Peasant, 32
Sun-Dried Tomato and Olive, 38

white flour, getting "good dough" with,
27
whole-grain breads:
    making in bread machine, 70
    see also whole-wheat breads
whole-grain flours, stone-ground, 18
    getting "good dough" with, 27–28
whole-wheat breads, 55–67
    Carrot-Orange, 62
    Cherry, Walnut, and Vanilla, 64
    Cinnamon, Raisin, and Walnut,
    74
    Honey, 56
    Honey (bread machine), 72
    Honey-Oat, 66

whole-wheat breads (*cont'd*)
    Mushroom, Parsley, and Jack Cheese,
    58
    Pizza (bread machine), 76
    Seven-Grain (bread machine), 73
    Swiss and Spinach, 60
wooden spoons, 22

yeast, 18–19
    active dry, 18–19
    in bread-machine breads, 70
    fresh or compressed, 18
    instant dried, 19
    oven spring and, 25
    quick-rise, 19

About the Author

Cindi Flahive-Sobel and her husband, Scott, moved their five children from Colorado to Boston to open the first of the Boston Daily Bread Bakeries. While Cindi became a master baker and built a thriving consulting business, Scott stayed home with the kids. There are now two Boston Daily Bread Bakeries in the Boston area, and more than twenty bakeries across the country who use Cindi's delicious whole-grain recipes and espouse her bread-baking philosophy. Cindi lives with her husband and children in Sudbury, Massachusetts, and divides her time between the stores and traveling for her consulting business.

Metric Equivalencies

LIQUID AND DRY MEASURE EQUIVALENCIES

Customary	Metric
¼ teaspoon	1.25 milliliters
½ teaspoon	2.5 milliliters
1 teaspoon	5 milliliters
1 tablespoon	15 milliliters
1 fluid ounce	30 milliliters
¼ cup	60 milliliters
⅓ cup	80 milliliters
½ cup	120 milliliters
1 cup	240 milliliters
1 pint (2 cups)	480 milliliters
1 quart (4 cups, 32 ounces)	960 milliliters (.96 liter)
1 gallon (4 quarts)	3.84 liters
1 ounce (by weight)	28 grams
¼ pound (4 ounces)	114 grams
1 pound (16 ounces)	454 grams
2.2 pounds	1 kilogram (1000 grams)

OVEN TEMPERATURE EQUIVALENCIES

Description	°Fahrenheit	°Celsius
Cool	200	90
Very slow	250	120
Slow	300–325	150–160
Moderately slow	325–350	160–180
Moderate	350–375	180–190
Moderately Hot	375–400	190–200
Hot	400–450	200–230
Very hot	450–500	230–260